This book is dedicated to my son,
Matthew Rhodes

The Little Embryo That Could

Conquering Genetic Termination, Secondary Infertility, and Other Setbacks

Suzanne Harris Rhodes

Published by:
Suzanne H. Rhodes

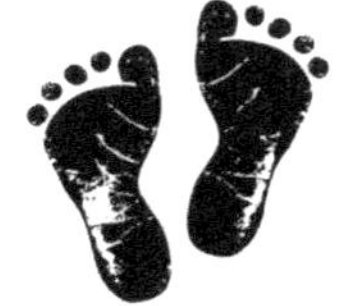

www.suzannehrhodes.com

ISBNs:
978-0-578-36949-5 (print)
978-0-578-36950-1 (ebook)

The names of some characters in the book
have been changed to protect identity.

The content of this book is not intended to replace
medical advice with respect to infertility.

Cover and interior design by Gary A. Rosenberg
Editing by Candace Johnson, Change It Up Editing
All poetry is the author's original work.

Good things come to those who wait

~Unknown

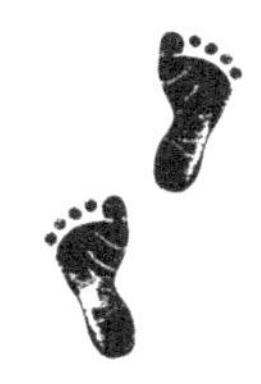

Contents

Author's Note...ix

Introduction.................................... 1

Chapter 1. Tommy's Story............................5

Chapter 2. Bad Luck Events...........................25

Chapter 3. More Bad Luck............................53

Chapter 4. Enough Bad Luck Already!...............68

Chapter 5. New Challenges..........................87

Chapter 6. The IVF Party........................... 109

Chapter 7. Losing It......................... 131

Chapter 8. More IVF......................... ... 146

Chapter 9. Nirvana 157

Chapter 10. Matthew's Birth Story.................. 179

Chapter 11. Icing on the Cake...................... 189

Chapter 12. Gifts and Lessons Learned 194

Acknowledgments 201

Terms and Acronyms.............................. 203

Support and Resources 209

About the Author............................... 211

Author's Note

I have included dated entries throughout the book of my correspondence to various members of two message boards, A Heartbreaking Choice (AHC), for women who terminated pregnancies due to fetal anomalies, and Subsequent Pregnancy Discussion (SPD), for women who were pregnant following such a previous termination.

Introduction

This journey we call life takes many unexpected twists and turns, and every now and then, a series of wrong turns will lead to a pot of gold in the end. This book is about hardship, and also about the rewards life has to offer if one perseveres.

When I look at my son, I get teary-eyed at times. I feel like I am dreaming—his existence seems surreal. I never thought I would be sitting here looking at this towheaded, blue-eyed miracle who melts my heart every time I look at him. Many mothers take their children for granted, but not me. I have been given a gift beyond comparison, and I walked through the furnace to get it. I want to share my story with others to give them grounds for hope.

A couple of months before trying to conceive, I cut out all alcohol and weaned off my antidepressant medication, Prozac, to be on the safe side. I have suffered from chronic clinical depression since my late twenties. It runs in my family, and if I stay on the medication, I function sufficiently—but when I'm not on it, I cry almost daily for no reason at all, even when things are going peachy in my life. I was ashamed for many years to have this condition, but now I realize it's something beyond my control and that I am in good company—millions of others struggle with depression too.

It was July of 2000, and life was good. I convinced my husband, Mark, to have a third child after much effort. In a few months, our family would be complete. Simple enough.

It took several months of consideration to talk Mark into having another baby, as he did not share my enthusiasm for having more than two kids. He values his free time, and he is a fan of order and is not into noise and commotion as I am. I thrive on existence with animals and kids in my orbit who need and love me without condition—an engaging, boisterous household full of life. I couldn't get rid of that maternal drive to have another child. An inexplicable urge built inside me like a tidal wave that could not be suppressed.

I already had two beautiful daughters, Ally and Deborah, ages two and eleven. Their age span was so broad because my oldest daughter resulted from my first marriage six years earlier. I conceived my daughters without incident, each on the first attempt. The pregnancies were routine and uneventful. I was a baby-making machine.

With my first daughter, Deborah, I had an old-fashioned doctor who did not believe in doing sonograms, and at fourteen weeks, I declined the alpha-fetoprotein (AFP) test, which checks for Down syndrome and spina bifida. I was pretty much in the dark about my baby's well-being—I went on blind faith that everything would be okay. After all, I was just twenty-three years old at the time of my first pregnancy.

Pregnant again at thirty-three with my second daughter, Ally, I declined the amniocentesis. After all, horrific things like that only happened to other people. If there had been a problem, I would not have terminated the pregnancy anyway.

Lucky for me, both girls were born healthy. I loved them so much, but I took it for granted that I had two healthy children—that's just the way things were supposed to be. I had no idea of the events in store for my third child.

Let the games begin! The reproduction started in earnest. As you may know, baby-making sex is not a fun endeavor—it's a *chore*. ("Okay, honey, I'm ovulating—we have to do it *now*. I don't care if the Bears are in overtime against the Packers.")

Afterward, I would lay on my back with my legs over my head for twenty minutes to ensure none of those spermies escaped their fate. No "smoking a cigarette afterward/basking in nirvana" scenario for me.

Trisomy 13 was a condition I never considered.

CHAPTER 1

Tommy's Story

Where can you scream? It's a serious question:
where can you go in society and scream?
~R. D. Laing

The jangle of the phone pumped my adrenaline into high gear. The professional on the other end possessed a life-changing verdict. My nerves had buzzed all morning as I anticipated this call, the minutes slipping along like creeping slugs. I hoped beyond hope for good news.

I snatched up the receiver and answered with hesitation.

"Hello, is this Ms. Rhodes?"

"Yes, this is she," I answered.

"This is Dr. Bowers." The doctor himself calling instead of the nurse was never a good sign in my book. "I'm calling to let you know the results of your amniocentesis are in, and they confirm full trisomy 13, plus an additional marker chromosome."

This was when my out-of-body experience occurred. I gazed down upon a woman clutching the phone who was in a state of frenzy, releasing a series of feral, hysterical screams that sounded like a lioness witnessing the murder of her cherished cub. *Who is that unfortunate creature?* I thought. *It can't be me.* In an instant, I catapulted back into my body, and the horror of my life took hold. My mother, who was visiting at the time, seized the receiver in a protective gesture and demanded the geneticist give her names and phone numbers of doctors who could "take care of this."

I crumpled into a sobbing heap on the bed. This is the stuff pregnant women's nightmares are made of, where their subconscious fears surface in the dream world. In my case, the nightmare materialized.

I had beamed when the pregnancy test registered positive after just the second month of trying. I had two daughters and desired a third child to complete my family. Many of my friends were already pregnant or trying, so this was an exciting time of "pregnancy bonding" with them, sharing tales of morning sickness and discussing due dates. I was one month shy of thirty-six when I got pregnant; I was still in the "safe zone" in terms of age.

I met Mark while working for a telecommunications firm a short time after my divorce. We ran into each other at a bar one night, started dating in 1994, and married in 1996. At the beginning of our marriage, I had one eight-year-old daughter, Deborah, from my previous marriage. Mark and I agreed not to expand our family any further. However, a year later, we decided to have a child together; in 1998, our daughter, Alexandra, was born. Then in 2000, my maternal desires ignited once again, and I begged and pleaded for one final child.

Mark, who was then thirty-six, did not want another baby, but I wore him down with my persistent pleas. He did not want the additional work, stress, and financial burden that another child would entail. He has a type-A personality and worries about the practicalities of everything while I tend to be more laid back.

Right on schedule, my morning sickness set in at six weeks.

I remember feeling exhausted, even more tired than I'd felt in my previous pregnancies, as if I had the flu. I told people that something was different about this pregnancy. I convinced myself I was carrying more than one. With each pregnancy, I'd fantasized about having twins. My mother delivered twin boys when she was thirty-seven, and at eleven years old, I derived endless enjoyment from helping my parents with the day-to-day child-rearing duties. At this point in my life some twenty-five years later, I craved a large family.

My first obstetrical appointment was at eight weeks, and Dr. Grimes asked, "Do you plan on having an amniocentesis at around sixteen weeks?" Without hesitation, I said, "No. I don't want to risk a miscarriage, and, if the baby has Down syndrome, I plan on having him/her anyway." The good doctor went on to paint a rosy picture of a high-functioning teenaged boy with Down syndrome who attended his church.

I had my second prenatal appointment at twelve weeks, and I was gratified to hear the heartbeat, a reassuring milestone. Hearing the gallop of your tiny baby's heart for the first time is an unequaled feeling of wonder and exhilaration. Dr. Hart, another doctor in the practice, performed my exam that day. She pulled out the tape and measured my swollen belly. "Your uterus is measuring slightly larger than normal for your dates," she said.

"Twins run in my family," I said, my excitement building. "I have fraternal twin brothers. I've also felt a lot more tired than in my other pregnancies."

Given this new information, she decided: "Let's order an ultrasound to check for twins." I floated on a cloud of euphoria. I scheduled a sonogram appointment for one week later, pleased that I could schedule one so soon.

On December 19, 2000, the day of the sonogram, the sky had the cloudy, gray appearance of impending snow. We wondered if the weatherman's snowy forecast for the Washington, DC metro area would turn out to be another bust, as it had many times in the twenty-eight years I'd lived here.

Mark and I were anxious to find out if I was indeed carrying twins. On the drive over to Washington Radiology, we shared our differing viewpoints on the pluses and minuses of having twins.

"Oh, I hope it's twins!" I said.

Mark shook his head. "No way. One's enough." His pragmatic nature resonated. He did not want the financial burden of that many children or the additional work of a larger family.

After about thirty minutes in the waiting room, they called us in for the ultrasound. The technician made some calibrations on the machine, spread the cold jelly on my abdomen, and started moving the wand around in circular motions. Soon, she found the fetus in its fluid-filled sac. We saw the heartbeat flickering away. She announced that I was carrying just one baby. I was a little disappointed but not too much. I was just happy that my one baby appeared to be developing in a typical fashion.

The technician spent several minutes taking measurements of the fetus, and when she finished, she said, "The doctor will be in to see you in a minute." I was perplexed. I did not see a doctor after the ultrasound with my second child. Perhaps this was just the procedure at this particular lab. While we were waiting for the doctor, our eyes danced as we looked over the grainy sonogram images. We discussed whether we thought it was a boy or a girl. I did not care as long as the baby was healthy.

The doctor came in and started doing another sonogram. At this point, I was beginning to get nervous. After she finished, she told us, "There is a measurement of fluid on the back of the neck called the nuchal translucency, and your baby's is slightly higher than normal. Normal is up to 3.2 millimeters (mm), and your baby's is measuring 3.4 mm. This is a marker for Down syndrome." She reassured us this was just one marker, and it did not prove our baby had this abnormality. However, as any mother-to-be knows, anything deviating from typical causes concern. Adding to my distress, the due date was adjusted from June 24 to June 28, the date of my father's sudden death sixteen years prior.

Dread filled my gut like a lead ball. My fortress of happiness started to crumble—this news marked the beginning of my life coming apart. My doctor recommended that I have chorionic villus sampling (CVS) as soon as possible since my ultrasound indicated that I was already at twelve weeks and four days into my pregnancy, and the cutoff for CVS was thirteen weeks.

She slipped out of the room to write down the term *nuchal translucency* for us. When she returned, tears were pooling in my eyes. We exited through the waiting room. The hot lava of my emotions threatened to blow. With my red, weepy eyes, I am sure I did not personify the happy mother-to-be. The other pregnant mommies stole confused, nervous glances my way as I made a hasty departure. God knows what they thought when they saw me.

Fat snowflakes fell from the sky on the way home, an event that usually fills me with wonderment since I love the white powder as much as a child does. This time, however, it meant nothing. I stared out the car window at the snowflakes, oblivious to their appeal, as my husband drove home in silence. A dark cloud settled over me.

I first learned of Genetics and IVF Institute (GIVF) from Kate Baker, my friend and neighbor across the street. She worked there for several years as a lab supervisor. When the doctor suggested I get a CVS test based on my ultrasound findings, Kate advised me to go to GIVF, as they would have more expertise for this test. I researched GIVF on their website (www.givf.com) and was impressed: "World-renowned for its pioneering work in infertility and genetics, GIVF developed or perfected many of the treatments and techniques used today in other centers worldwide."

After the recommendation from Kate, I dialed GIVF and scheduled the CVS test for that Friday (December 22). My mother-in-law's flight to Washington, DC was arriving from Indiana for Christmas on Thursday night, so I knew I would have to maintain my composure. Doris visited just once a year, and I did not want to spoil her holidays with a negative disposition.

The night before the CVS, my stomach was a ball of swarming butterflies. I worried about the pain of the procedure; however, I agonized more about the possibility of miscarriage. Hours passed before I fell asleep.

At the genetics lab the next day, I almost declined the CVS when the genetics doctor told me that given my age and the nuchal measurement, there was a mere 1 percent chance of my baby having Down syndrome.

"Are you sure you still want to have it?" Dr. Bowers asked.

I pondered the question and then answered that I did. I knew that if I opted out of the test, the niggling doubt about the baby's health would eat away at me for the next six months of my pregnancy.

Mark stood guard at my head while I planted a death grip on his hand. The assisting nurse warned, "Your husband might want to take a seat. We once had a burly police officer pass out in here." Mark decided to take his chances and stand. The procedure produced little pain; I just felt pressure. Once the needle was inserted into my abdomen, it took about thirty seconds to draw out a sample of the chorionic villi from the placenta. I was relieved at the brevity of the process.

Dr. Bowers assured me the odds of Down syndrome were small; this statement did not mitigate my worries. But the situation obliterated my holiday spirit. After the CVS, I put myself on bed rest for the next two days, my conservative approach to prevent a miscarriage. I was relieved that I did not experience any cramping or bleeding from the procedure over the next several days.

The CVS test results were supposed to come back in seven to ten days. That did not happen. I started calling the lab after just six days elapsed. I was quite a nuisance. I called from time to time over the next several days, disappointed to get the same answer from the genetics counselor: "We're still waiting for the cells to grow."

On January 4, the genetics counselor told me that the cells did not grow on the first culture, so they would be put in for a reculture. I asked her if the failure of the cell growth might be a sign of a genetic problem, and she said, "Sometimes but not necessarily." This response amplified the doubt in my mind. She said that sometimes the reculture worked and sometimes it did not, and to check back early the following week. I burst into tears on the phone at the prospect of the CVS failing to produce results and having to go through a subsequent amnio (with another grueling wait and risk of miscarriage). This was the point when I started falling apart.

On Monday, January 8, when the cells still were not growing, I went ahead and scheduled a tentative amnio for that Friday (January 12). If the CVS results came back before Friday, I would just cancel the amnio. I prayed that the cells from the CVS reculture would grow.

On Thursday, January 11, three unbearable weeks after my CVS, I received a call from the genetics doctor. Dr. Bowers said in a clinical tone, "Six of the cells finally grew, and we found two problems: Full trisomy 13 and an extra 'marker' chromosome." I was at home alone when I got the news, and I received it with uncharacteristic calm. I believe I was in shock, disbelief, and denial. The doctor went on to tell me that these two unrelated events together were so rare that they had never seen it in their genetics lab; the odds of this happening were astronomical. I'd hit the genetic lottery. Humans are supposed to have forty-six chromosomes—my baby had *forty-eight.*

"Do you know what trisomy 13 is?" he asked.

"Yes," I said. "The genetic counselor explained it to me in the pre-CVS counseling session, and I researched it on the internet." The counselor had described these two problems as a "genetic train wreck" and explained that the baby's condition would be so grave that he/she would not even have personality. The enormity of the situation tightened my chest with the pressure of a boa constrictor.

Dr. Bowers recommended that I still have the amnio the following day to confirm the result, given the circumstances of the slow-growing CVS cells. The genetics counselor then called and said that carrying this baby might jeopardize my health; due to the damaged cells in the placenta, I might have a placental abruption later in my pregnancy and bleed to death or get preeclampsia, a life-threatening condition in which your blood pressure elevates, and coma and death can result. She also said that in terms of emotional impact, it would be dangerous to my family to have a trisomy 13 baby.

TRISOMY 13

Trisomy 13 is a rare genetic abnormality where three chromosomes are on pair #13 instead of two. It occurs in one out of every five thousand births. The entire genetic coding is damaged and then propagated throughout every organ system in the body. Following are some of the manifestations:

- Brain defects (severe mental retardation)
- Severe eye defects (and sometimes blindness)
- Hearing problems (and malformed ears)
- Heart defects
- Genitourinary defects
- Gastrointestinal defects
- Cleft lip/palate
- Apneic spells (sudden interruption of breathing)
- Seizures
- Skeletal defects
- Skin defects
- Polydactyly (additional fingers and/or toes)

Most trisomy 13 babies die in utero before term or live (in pain) for only a few minutes, hours, or days after birth. Fewer than 20 percent survive beyond one year of age.

As if trisomy 13 were not bad enough, the doctor stated that the extra "marker" chromosome could have additional devastating consequences.

At this point, I decided I would terminate my pregnancy. Although I have always been pro-life and my religious convictions went against terminating, I felt this was the best outcome given two unfavorable situations.

On Friday, January 12, I went to Genetics and IVF Institute for the amnio. Beforehand, I burst into tears in the genetic counselor's office when I noted the "XY" code from the report on her desk, indicating a male. My dream was to have a boy and name him after my late father. While the technician performed the pre-amnio sonogram, my body convulsed with sobs.

"Can you please turn off the screen that's facing me?" I asked as I covered my eyes with my hand. The antiseptic smell of the exam room was nauseating. The doctor and technician proceeded to do a thorough level 2 sonogram (with their most sophisticated machine) for about forty-five minutes. They did not find any visual abnormalities (such as cleft lip/palate or smaller head measurement). The one thing the doctor found to be suspect was the fact that not once during the entire scan did he see the baby open his fists (trisomy 13 babies are so neurologically impaired that they can't do so). He stressed that this was a minor observation, though.

The genetic counselor told me that in some rare cases, just a portion of the placenta is damaged by trisomy 13, and the amnio goes on to indicate that the baby is not affected. This is called *placental mosaicism*. I held onto this tiny hope, coupled with the normal-looking sonogram, through the weekend.

However, I told myself not to build false hope. I researched "placental mosaicism" on the internet and printed out an excerpt stating that in 1 percent of cases, the CVS indicates a genetic problem with the fetus, but the problem turns out to be in only a portion of the placenta. I printed this, highlighted it, prayed that this was the case, and held onto it like a lifeline. An endless source of support, my mother stayed with us at our house through the weekend.

When the call came in on Monday morning, my worst fears were confirmed. My genetics counselor explained that since Virginia was such a conservative state on second-trimester abortions, we would have to travel to a Maryland abortion clinic to have the procedure. I was appalled that I could not have this done in a hospital, as I considered this to be a therapeutic abortion. She gave me a couple of names and phone numbers of doctors who performed terminations.

This was a no-win situation—if I decided to have the baby, I could be jeopardizing my life to deliver a baby that would live a short life filled with suffering. It seemed inhumane to me. If I aborted, I would have to live with this decision for the rest of my life. All I can say is that until you tread this rocky path, you do not know what you would do.

I called a clinic outside Baltimore that, to my relief, was able to give me an appointment that Wednesday. They explained it would be a two-day process for the dilation and evacuation (D&E). The actual procedure would be performed on Thursday.

As crazy as this may sound, a zany children's video called *Wee Sing Train* served as a silly diversion to get my mind off the looming termination of Tommy's pregnancy. My mother, who spent the night at our house before D-Day, commiserated with me on the couch while my two-year-old daughter, Ally, watched the video. Out of nowhere, this crazy, ridiculous character, Sheriff Knickerbocker, started dancing around with bowed legs like a rubber band man to the song "Hey, Mr. Knickerbocker, Boppity-Bop." My mother and I just looked at each other and started cracking up. This brief respite added an injection of light to an otherwise hopeless situation.

I cannot explain the agony that I felt during that week from the initial CVS results of trisomy 13 until the termination procedure. I was already feeling the baby move, and I would sit in my rocking chair at night with my hand on my stomach, praying to my baby and telling him how sorry I was. At all times, the palms of my hands and soles of my feet were wet from nerves. I was afraid of the procedure (especially at my advanced stage of pregnancy—seventeen weeks) and had never been put under anesthesia. I feared I would never wake up or that I'd suffer serious complications, a punishment for my decision.

On Wednesday morning, my mother, husband, and I set off on our clandestine road trip to Maryland. I felt like a "dead man walking," awaiting an execution. I anticipated there would be picketers outside the building; there were none, a small concession. We entered the tall, nondescript office building that housed the clinic, signed in with the receptionist, and were instructed to sit in a large waiting area. My eyes scanned numerous metal chairs against barren walls lining the perimeter of the cheerless space. The majority of the seats contained sullen teenagers.

It did not take long for me, someone who masks my emotions in public, to start sobbing in front of everyone. I ambled over to the front of the receptionist's desk, and she handed me some tissues and said, "I know how hard this is. You can wait in a second, more private, waiting room." I was impressed by her warmth and compassion. Perhaps she had "been there" herself, and that's why she took the job. She added that if the second waiting area was not private enough, my family and I could wait in an isolated room. I opted for the second waiting room.

I remember bawling into my tissues as several teenagers watched me leaving the first room. Nobody else was even crying. One of the girls appeared to be no more than fourteen years old. No one else appeared pregnant; my stomach protruded like a melon. I wondered if they thought I was a monster.

After I filled out some paperwork, I was called into a small room where a male technician with cornrows took a blood sample via a painful finger prick, the beginning of many punishments to come. Next, we walked down the hall to talk to the counselor, who explained the procedures. She gave me a strong dose of Motrin for the laminaria insertion that would soften my cervix in preparation for the next day's procedure.

Afterward, I went into a small room and met the doctor who would perform the procedure. She was a masculine woman who radiated compassion and competence. The doctor and nurse instructed me to lie down while they inserted the laminaria tents. As they placed them, I realized there was no turning back; this set the process in motion to end my baby's life. The procedure itself produced little pain. They told me I might have some cramping overnight, but I was spared that side effect.

We booked a room at a local hotel and tried to occupy our time by seeing a Julia Roberts movie at a local mall and eating dinner out at a restaurant. I was instructed not to eat or drink after 10:00 p.m. since I would be under heavy IV sedation, where I would still breathe on my own but have no recollection of the procedure. I scheduled my procedure for eight o'clock the next morning since I have hypoglycemia and cannot go long without food.

At the hotel, we got an adjoining suite with my mother. My husband and I slept in separate beds, as the beds did not have much room. That night, I lay in bed, unable to submit to the escape of sleep. I laid my hands on my stomach and prayed and blessed my baby. I was still aware of his movement.

I awoke at 5:30 the following morning, a bundle of nerves, and crawled into bed with my husband. "I'm scared," I said in a weak voice.

"Me too," he said. Deep sadness and fear enveloped us as we held each other.

I will never forget feeling my baby kicking for the last time as we sat at the traffic light on the corner where we were to turn into the clinic. All I can say is that it was pure hell.

After waiting about forty-five minutes, I was called in to begin the procedure. The nurse and doctor spoke in soft, reassuring tones. They led me into a regular examination room (I was surprised it was not an operating room). I remember calming music playing in the background (from *The Big Chill* soundtrack). The anesthesia nurse inserted an IV into my arm, delivering morphine and midazolam, and soon after, a chill snaked up the side of my throat.

"Is this normal for my throat to be cold?" I asked.

"Yes, the chill in your throat is normal," she said.

The last thing I remember is telling the doctor in a drunken state, "Thank you for helping me…" Then, I was out.

A short time later, I was pulled up by a nurse into a wheelchair and aroused from a groggy sleep. She wheeled me into a recovery room to lie down. Several teenagers and one older woman lay on cots.

My doctor came to my bedside and told me in a gentle voice, "You definitely did the right thing—your baby had six digits (fingers) on one hand, seven digits on the other hand, and six digits (toes) on each foot." She told me they had copies of the hand and footprints if I ever wanted them.

"Yes," I said without hesitation, "I do want them." I owed it to my baby to keep his prints.

My husband came to see me for a few minutes in recovery, but he left because more patients were coming in. I remained there for almost an hour, sipping ginger ale and eating graham crackers. I talked to a thirty-two-year-old woman who just terminated. I do not know what her circumstances were. She seemed nonchalant about the whole thing—maybe she was in shock.

I have a recollection of a small chapel across the street, directly in front of our car as we backed out of the parking space. The church stared back at me, recriminating eyes boring into my conscience. *God, please forgive me for what I just did,* I begged. My life would never be the same from this day forward, January 18, 2001.

Following the procedure, my bleeding was not heavy, and I never experienced any physical pain whatsoever. This was a blessing since the mental pain I endured both before and after the ordeal was enormous.

I siphoned off some of my emerging anger by wadding

up and trashing my treasures from the obstetrician's office in a tearful rage: my pregnancy pamphlets and a complimentary copy of *American Baby* magazine. My milk made an entrance three days after the termination, a harsh reminder that there was no baby to feed. The engorgement was painful in an emotional as well as physical manner. I lay in bed with a makeshift icepack of frozen peas draped across my chest, feeling useless and empty inside, a stocked grocery shelf with no customer in sight. This destroyed me.

Four days after the termination, I gathered the courage to look at my baby's hand- and footprints. I was amazed at how tiny they appeared, like a raccoon's. Seeing them was not as traumatic as I thought it would be, although rather emotional. I felt I owed it to my son to do this. As I ran my fingertips over the prints, I felt a tangible connection to my baby: his actual hands and feet had touched that paper.

The month following the termination was a blur of depression and despair. My husband took over all household duties (including diaper changes for our toddler) while I sat in the house and watched TV. For a solid month, I left the safety of my home on rare occasions. At times, I wished I were dead. My grief was an ocean: vast, boundless, constant. I was an empty shell, a zombie just going through the motions of breathing. This event razed the depths of my soul; I was not sure I could ever be recovered from this abyss.

Another cathartic outlet was transferring my feelings to paper. The tribute (poem) I wrote to Tommy soon after I lost him helped me sort out my emotions. Writing and sharing with my perinatal loss support group the complete account of my trisomy 13 experience also aided in the healing process, giving meaning to the tragedy.

Shattered

Once a lily in bloom, now a scattered mass of dead petals.

Shadows in my eyes, reflecting my anguish.

Misery beyond words.

Earth-shattering, mind-blowing, palpable torment.

So begins my catapult into the vortex of unrelenting darkness.

My once-beating heart, now a burned-out cavern in the earth,
*   with remnants of wreckage smoldering in the aftermath.*

My conscience unbearable, abysmal pain.

My God, how it hurts.

Will I ever recover?

I would notice towheaded toddler boys in the mall play area, tear up, and imagine what my son would have looked like. I named my son Thomas Harris Rhodes (Tommy) after my late father.

Three months after my loss, I called my genetics counselor, and she sent me the full medical report of the test results and the final sonogram pictures. I placed these in a wooden keepsake box on top of my dresser along with copies of the other sonogram pictures, the positive pregnancy test stick, and the hand- and footprints, a shrine to my tiny son.

On Tommy's due date of June 28 (also the sixteenth anniversary of my father's passing), my mother and I drove to Truro Episcopal Church in Fairfax, Virginia, which my family attended as I was growing up. We walked into the churchyard where my dad's ashes were scattered. We decided this would be the most meaningful place to hold our ceremony.

We tied together two blue balloons—one with Tommy's poem attached and the other with a short eulogy I wrote to my dad soon after his death—and released them. I felt that Tommy and my father were linked together and would be united in heaven. Parallel tragedies in my life, the deaths of my father and Tommy, were equidistant in their sharp entry points to my heart. One of the balloons found its way to a thorny branch of a tree, much to my dismay. "Mom—look! It's stuck!" I jumped up and down trying to free it and was afraid it would pop. I prayed for it to release, and it did when it was ready. I like to think of the symbolism in this—that it was Tommy's balloon lingering because he was not ready to say goodbye just yet.

On the solemn drive home, I willed the Sara MacLachlan song "I Will Remember You" to pour through the speakers. Even today, the lyrics portray my feelings and experience of Tommy's loss in an uncanny manner, like a dart hitting dead center; they speak to me on an emotional level. Much to my chagrin, the song did not play on the car ride that day, so my heartstrings were not strummed. On the rare occasion when I am privileged enough to have the song wash over me like a gentle saltwater wave, it is sacred, healing, and redefines my connection to my lost child. This ballad is my tribute and theme song for Tommy.

After I lost Tommy, I received a glass angel ornament from my perinatal loss counselor, Tina, and I bought a Snowbabies collectible angel. One of the same wings later broke off on each one. I felt this was providential: two physical angels had broken while the spiritual angel was whole and soaring, like Tommy.

Transferring my feelings to paper proved to be a cathartic outlet.

I wrote this tribute poem in honor of my son Tommy soon after his death, which helped me sort out my emotions:

ODE TO TOMMY

Although I never met you,
I knew you in my soul.
And I will not forget you,
It's my eternal goal.

I said if I ever had a boy,
I'd name him after dear ole dad.
The genetic tests removed that joy,
The prognosis was extremely bad.

Before I had to say goodbye,
I'd rock at night in my rocking chair.
"I wish you didn't have to fly,"
I'd tell you in a heartfelt prayer.

My garden, once in fullest bloom,
Empty, forlorn, devoid of life,
Now lies down in an empty tomb
At every turn, I discover strife.

Forgive me for what I had to do, I did it out of love.
Hopefully, Almighty God will, too,
As he smiles down from above.

Please know this, dear sweet little boy,
That one day we shall meet.
At that time I will feel pure joy,
My heart will be complete.

Mommy

CHAPTER 2

Bad Luck Events

If at first you don't succeed, try, try again.
~Thomas H. Palmer

Over the next three years, my life resembled the lyrics of a "down on your luck" country-western song. Pardon the expression, but I was a shit magnet. Under normal circumstances, I am not a superstitious person, but at times, I believed my never-ending streak of bad luck was the consequence of breaking those pesky internet chain letters we all loathe. When you read through these unfortunate events, you will think I am fabricating at least some of this, as this much misfortune could not befall one person in such rapid succession. However, I assure you that I have documented proof of every single heinous incident.

In February 2001, one month after my pregnancy termination, my two-and-one-half-year-old daughter, Ally, came down with pneumonia. She ran high fevers, and getting her to ingest the necessary antibiotics was like trying to give a rabid lion a haircut. It was a two-person operation: one to restrain her and another to attempt in vain to administer the nasty antidote without her regurgitating 100 percent of the contents. I performed this exercise three times a day, and it left me feeling like I'd just conducted an exorcism on Regan from *The Exorcist*.

They say what does not kill you makes you stronger, and this applied to my marriage as well. It is amazing that our marriage survived these four years of hell; I compare it to a beachfront home on stilts withstanding a Category 4 hurricane. Miraculously, although a few shingles were torn off and some windows shattered, in the end, the main structure was left standing. In the long run, we have grown closer from this ordeal, but there were many rough patches along the way.

❦

I do not remember how I stumbled upon the website A Heartbreaking Choice (AHC). I believe it was listed in the back of a grief pamphlet I received from my perinatal loss counselor. This website, which contains a message board designated for the unfortunate few who have made the heart-wrenching decision to terminate an unhealthy pregnancy, was my lifeline.

My first posting to the board, one month after losing Tommy, was my self-introduction.

Sunday, February 25, 2001

Hello. I'm new to this group. I had my much-wanted pregnancy terminated at seventeen weeks due to trisomy 13 and an extra "marker" chromosome (two unrelated events with devastating consequences). I was told by the genetics counselor that to carry the baby would jeopardize my health (risk of placental abruption/eclampsia). However, I would have terminated anyway (I felt it inhumane to bring my baby into the world with so many severe mental/ physical problems, only [for him] to suffer and die shortly after birth, or before birth). I have two girls already (ages twelve and two-and-a-half) and thought it would be really nice to have a boy and name him after my father, who died sixteen yrs. ago. As it turns out, the baby was a boy. I named him Thomas Harris (Tommy) after my father. I had a D&E versus induction of labor since I was under twenty weeks pregnant. I was put to sleep for the procedure. I now regret that I have no ashes to bury. I felt that terminating the pregnancy was the lesser of two evils. It's not fair that anyone should be faced with this decision. I never thought I would. I had my pregnancy terminated on Jan. 18, 2001. My due date would have been June 28, 2001 (ironically, the date that my dad died sixteen yrs. ago). I hope that the significance of this date means that my dad is now watching over Tommy in heaven. I am so sad. I have okay days and bad ones. This is one of the bad ones. Life is just so unfair sometimes! Almost all of my friends are pregnant or have just had babies, and this cuts through me like a knife (even though I'm happy for them). I really want another child, but don't know if I could go through this again. I'm afraid this or Down syndrome would happen next time (I'm thirty-six yrs. old). The genetics counselor said I have a one-in-100 chance of a chromosome problem next time. I just hope that I can eventually find some happiness in life! I did exercise today, which was a monumental effort. I'm still carrying some of the pregnancy weight, so still have to wear my maternity pants (really depressing)! Then, when I get depressed, I pig out! A vicious cycle!!! Oh well—sorry this is so long. Reading the other stories on this board is helping me out (although I wish you all didn't have to go through this, like me)!

Are there any other T-13s on this board?

☙

Within the confines of my computer, merely keystrokes away, I found a camaraderie of other survivors of this ordeal, a safe haven to retreat to and pour out my feelings, to drain some of the venom from my snakebite.

The anomalies that women on this board lost their babies to were vast, including Down syndrome (trisomy 21), Patau syndrome (trisomy 13), Edwards syndrome (trisomy 18), severe heart defects, anencephaly, and Dandy-Walker syndrome, to name a few.

I will never forget the first woman I "met" electronically who lost a baby to the same anomaly as mine—trisomy 13. She lived all the way in Australia. I was consoled when I found her. It felt like finding a needle in a haystack. Being able to correspond with her was a balm to my wound. Little did I know that over the course of the next several months, I would discover many more trisomy 13 pregnancy survivors on this godsend of a website.

I was misfortunate enough to learn a great deal about the myriad of things that can go awry in a pregnancy. Many of the syndromes I had never even heard of. I acquired enough knowledge from this website to practically become a genetics counselor. Reading these entries was not for the thin-skinned or those with a weak constitution. These were raw, frontline accounts of tragedy, of life at its worst. A couple of the unfortunate members even terminated *two* of their pregnancies due to anomalies. I tried to remember that when I started to feel sorry for myself.

My mother, though, thought that my obsession with this site was detrimental to me and that I was feeding my depression by conversing with these people. What she did not understand was that it was just what I needed at the time. I was an active member of the site for seven months, from February 2001 (one month past my pregnancy interruption) until September 2001 (one month after my first miscarriage). It served its purpose until I was ready to stop focusing on the pain of my termination, embark on a healthy future pregnancy, and move on.

❧

Before the great baby debate, Mark and I got along like a pair of turtle doves, except for the occasional tiffs over common issues like money. I call it the "baby debate"—I wanted another one, and Mark did not. He didn't want the work, expenses, and time another child would entail. He was scared senseless we would be faced with another chromosome issue in a subsequent pregnancy. This was a major stumbling block in our relationship.

Thursday, March 8, 2001

Well, every time one of our daughters starts acting up, my husband says, 'I can't believe you want another baby!' Also, he says that it depresses him to have that hanging over his head. This is about the only thing we ever argue about. It's causing a major issue in our relationship. He's a great husband and father—he just doesn't want any more kids. I wish I could just get rid of this yearning that I have in me for another one, but I can't.

❧

At times, I feared Mark would leave me over this, but I persisted. I knew the pain would eat me alive if I did not get my baby in the end. I was willing to risk it all to achieve this.

Thursday, April 26, 2001
Unfortunately, my DH [dear husband] doesn't share my enthusiasm (an understatement) about TTC [trying to conceive] again. He just kind of grudgingly agreed to it. I feel guilty about that, too. How can I be so selfish to want to have another baby when he doesn't? I just can't explain my desire to have another child. It's just very strong, and I can't control it. I don't want to end my childbearing years with AHC [the term for a pregnancy termination due to fetal anomalies] as my last memory.

❧

It was a cruel fate that during the time I lost Tommy, I was in a playgroup for my daughter, Ally, then two-and-one-half years old, with six other pregnant women. They all had due dates within a couple months of Tommy's.

After not attending meetings for a month, I resumed going, an effort to recapture some normalcy in my routine. I must hand it to them—they did refrain from discussing their pregnancies in front of me as much as possible, but I felt like my presence detracted from their joy. I knew they wanted to talk pregnancy and babies (who wouldn't?), but my attendance hindered them. This made me feel like a pariah; I stood out like a sore thumb.

This was an isolating time for me, and I retreated to the comfort of my internet support boards as a reprieve in the evenings, airing my feelings of discontent. Receiving the inevitable plethora of baby shower invitations from the playgroup moms months later (that I would never attend) was disconcerting, and I envied their circumstances.

Thursday, March 8, 2001

To top it off, four of my friends recently had babies, and six of my friends in my toddler's playgroup are currently pregnant. I actually went to the playgroup today (had gone another time a couple of weeks ago since my AHC). The first time I went, it didn't bother me too much, but this time it upset me. One of the women pulled me to the side and secretly told me about a baby shower for two of the women on April 21. That's what did it for me! I started getting really depressed and angry (after I got home), and my day is ruined! Needless to say, I will send presents but will not be attending the shower. I'd probably break down in tears!

✑

Our family's bad karma continued. My husband, Mark, worked for Media Centers, one of a myriad of telecommunications start-up companies that cropped up at that time. This one specialized in fiber-optic transport. He took a gamble by leaving his safe government position to work at this company but felt it could turn out to be lucrative as well as a tremendous learning opportunity.

Tensions were running high in the Rhodes household because of the recent loss of our baby and the precarious footing of the new company. Media Centers was awaiting critical funding from their capital investor to keep them afloat. At the time, I worked part-time at Sprint in Reston, Virginia, and we were aware that we could not make ends meet on my salary alone.

Humor was a vital coping mechanism during the heavy times. My ability to attract myself to despondent situations was uncanny. I marveled at my astronomical odds: considering I was the one-in-a-million statistic, according to my genetics counselor (tri 13 alone is one in 5000 at my age, but tri 13 *and* an additional marker chromosome is the one-in-a-million jackpot)! I told her, "Why couldn't I be that lucky with the lottery?" I tried to find humor—it was sometimes the only thing that got me through.

The big day arrived that would determine the fate of the new company, and, wouldn't you know it, *they did not get the funding*. Mark arrived home that evening in April 2001 (three months after the pregnancy termination) and delivered the fantastic news that he was now jobless and without any severance pay. Of course, I dissolved into tears. The good times just kept on rolling.

Thursday, April 26, 2001

I just need to vent. I feel like my life just stinks! My AHC [pregnancy termination] was three months ago, then my 2½ yr. old had pneumonia, and now my DH is about to lose his job any day now (he works for a start-up telecom company that's about to go under—can't get funding). I'm not sure how we'll be able to pay our mortgage, food, etc. The tensions are running high right now between my DH and me. I don't mean to be a complainer, but I can't take much more of this. I'm on a 40mg a day dose of Prozac and was doing okay until about a week ago. Now, I feel like that's not even going to work anymore. I feel like burying my head under the sand and not coming out until the storm passes. I feel guilty even writing this 'cause I know there are others on this AHC board with greater problems than I. I just need to get it off my chest before I explode!!

⁊

I developed an unhealthy obsession with a trisomy 13 online support board. I was hoping to find other kindred spirits who also made the painful decision to end their trisomy 13 pregnancies so we could commiserate. Instead, most of the entries were filled with messages from brave mothers who chose to continue their pregnancies.

Despite my findings, I continued to torture myself by frequenting this board, often late at night when I felt intense desperation. It was detrimental for me to read these entries, as doing so generated a great deal of guilt over my decision.

I recall following one message thread about a child, referred to as the "Amazing Hayden," stricken with both trisomy 13 and trisomy 18 and thriving. This caused me to question my decision. Perhaps Tommy could have been like Hayden and defied the odds. In turn, my wound, loosely stitched in guilt, reopened and oozed with blood and self-loathing.

I knew in my rational mind that visiting this message board was not healthy for me. I suppose I was trying to further punish myself in a subconscious manner for my irreversible decision, one which I would have to live with until my final breath.

Tuesday, May 1, 2001
I know what you mean about the T-18 boards. I find the T-13 board to be just as unsettling. I finally had to stop going on it because it was making me feel like such a horrible person! We did prevent our babies from a short life that would have been filled with suffering (for them as well as our families), though!

❧

After the birth of my friend Cristin's baby, Vance, I decided to be strong and force myself to visit her in the hospital post-delivery. She was one of the numerous friends from Ally's playgroup who was pregnant at the same time I was supposed to be pregnant with Tommy. Vance was born in May 2001, one month before Tommy was to have been born. This was a significant step for me, the first effort on my part to incorporate myself into the world of "New Happy Mothers with Babies," a club I was not a part of.

I entered her hospital room playing the part without a hitch: bearing gifts, telling her how beautiful her son was as he lay across the bed before her like a cherub. Little did she know that, inside, I was dying.

❧

My mother, siblings, and I decided a four-day trip to the Bahamas would serve as a once-in-a-lifetime chance to travel together as a nuclear family. My sister, Karen, and I were fortunate enough to marry kindhearted, generous men who were willing to carry the load while we took a well-deserved break (my sister has five children, so it goes without saying that she needed some time to herself). My twin brothers, Tim and Chris, both twenty-four years old at the time and unencumbered, were more than game to accommodate our wishes and join us for this adventure. Such good sports. Tim, the consummate traveler, took charge and booked us, landing a stellar deal that May.

This trip was just what I needed at the time (four months after losing Tommy to trisomy 13) to escape my demons and enter a fantasy world where grief could not coexist with joyous abandon.

Upon arrival at the all-inclusive resort, we initiated our sabbatical by ordering piña coladas with those cute little umbrellas while we reclined in chaise lounges. "This is the life," I mused.

The first night, feeling a lack of inhibition and a little euphoria after a few Amstel Lights, I stood out on our hotel room balcony and belted out the song, "Who Let the Dogs Out." I thought it was hilarious and that my fellow travelers lucky enough to be within earshot would feel the same.

My mom ventured downstairs to order a drink at the bar (undoubtedly to get a brief reprieve from the vocal entertainment) and came back to the hotel room about forty-five minutes later, shaking her head with a dual expression of censure and amusement. She said, "I was downstairs in the bar talking to a gentleman, and he complained that some teenager next door to his room was singing some song about dogs, and he had to change rooms to get some peace and quiet. I was thinking, *That was my thirty-seven-year-old daughter.*" Indeed, one of my finer moments.

Most of our time was spent in such hedonistic activities as

sunning poolside with slushy alcoholic drinks, going out to eat at cheerful multicolored restaurants, swimming and laying out on the beach, and of course the infamous "booze cruise." No Caribbean vacation would be complete without a rum cruise, would it?

The sales pitch for the booze cruise involved a Bahamian man bouncing over to us with zeal as we lay out on the beach and shouting, "Booze cruise! You spill it, we fill it! You drop it, we mop it!" He made us an offer we could not refuse.

So, we set out down the beach at the appointed hour, decked out in our island garb and ready to party. As all booze cruises commence, the first sober hour or so, people spoke in hushed tones among themselves, keeping to their own conservative groups.

However, as the rum punch (*strong* rum punch, I might add) started flowing freely and was ingested at ever-increasing rates in the blistering sun, the lines among the clans became blurred, and I found myself in an animated conversation with just about anyone who would listen. Well into the cruise, I acquired several new "best friends" who I requested, "Gimme five," hand slaps from every few minutes. I am a shy person around new groups of people, but I found myself shouting, "Hey, Bahama Mama!" to one of the women serving rum punch on the lower deck and playing matchmaker for my brother, Chris, with a new blonde girl I met.

After the cruise concluded, the party continued in the resort pool after my brother, Tim, scored a bottle of rum and a liter jug of Coca-Cola (the rules are rather lax in the Bahamas). We met and partied with two new "best buds" in the pool, a couple from Newark, New Jersey, who had also just stepped off the infamous cruise.

Later that evening, I dared my brother Tim to take a dip in the decorative fountain outside the hotel. He obliged, of course. My sister, Karen, brother Chris, and I joined him in short order. My mother just stood aside in incredulity at our antics. By the grace of God, the hotel management did not witness our fountain follies.

This wild and frivolous holiday, however outrageous, was just what I needed at the time to help ease my heart's burden.

❦

After losing Tommy to trisomy 13, I felt as isolated as a diamond in a garbage dump. I had never heard of anyone who experienced such a rare chromosomal problem with their pregnancy. I was a freak, a leper stranded on my own island, with no one to turn to who could appreciate or fathom what I was going through.

Two weeks after the devastating loss, I began to see a peri-natal loss counselor who my genetics counselor recommended. I will never forget my first impression of her. She was wearing a snow-white fuzzy angora sweater that gave her a cherubic aura. Her abundant compassion was reflected in her countenance. It was as if a guardian angel dropped out of heaven to help carry me through my despair. She confided that she experienced the loss of twins many years earlier and could relate to my pain. She told me I would have to walk through it, but that I would see the light at the end of the tunnel at some point in the future. I held onto that hope like a lifeline.

We worked through my grief and my husband's resistance to trying again for another child and discussed the possibility of adoption. I lived for my weekly meetings and saw her for six months.

After most sessions, I drove home in tears that clouded my vision. One gloomy, rainy day, I felt at one with the elements, the gray sky opening and releasing its veil of tears. I hoped that at some point, I would be released from this prison of despondency.

In 2001, six months after my pregnancy termination, my counselor formed a small group of women, myself included, who interrupted their pregnancies due to various anomalies. We met on the last Thursday of each month in the evenings from 7:00–8:30 p.m. Ironically, the date of the first meeting was June 28, my due date with Tommy and the anniversary of my father's death, a date when I needed sustenance the most.

Lacey, in her early forties, experienced a Down syndrome pregnancy. Meg's baby had a condition called *omphalocele,* where the internal organs form outside the baby's body. Reema's baby suffered from severe heart defects and Joan's baby from Down syndrome.

We shared our stories with tears. Meeting with these women was therapeutic to my healing process, and I made some valuable friendships. Meg and Joan went on to deliver healthy babies, Lacey adopted a baby girl, and Reema pursued donor egg IVF.

❦

June 2001 brought more fun. My oldest daughter, Deborah, and her cousin, Liza, both twelve years old, attended a two-week-long camp at Camp Chanco in Southern Virginia. My former sister-in-law, Amy, drove us to the camp to pick up the girls without incident. I drove my car home from Amy's house in Springfield with my two girls. Ally was almost three years old at that time.

There was a steady rainfall outside, so the roads were slick. The traffic was backing up as we approached the stoplight at Route 50 and Pleasant Valley Road, a known problem area. We were approximately two miles from home, and both of my children were asleep.

The driver in front of me hit the brakes without warning, I jammed mine down, and the SUV behind me slammed into my midsize sedan, resulting in a charming seven-car pileup on Route 50. My glasses went sailing off my head onto the dashboard, and one of my flip-flops got wedged under the brake. I swung my head around to make sure my girls were okay. Deborah woke up from a sound sleep and screamed; her feet had bashed into a metal bar under her seat and were bleeding. My youngest was still slumbering in her car seat, and, at first, I thought she was unconscious.

The woman in the SUV behind me was frantic when she saw that my daughter was injured. I borrowed a cell phone to call my husband, and he arrived soon after. The back of our Chrysler Concorde looked like an accordion. The emergency crew arrived, and the paramedics placed Deborah on a backboard to be on the safe side and moved Ally, still in her car seat, to the ambulance. I accompanied my girls in the back of the ambulance to Fair Oaks Hospital.

Thank goodness, Deborah's foot wounds turned out to be superficial, and Ally's neurological tests checked out okay. We waited an interminable amount of time for the foot X-rays, spending about three hours of our evening in the hospital.

Then, of course, there was all the red tape involved in an

auto accident (police report, dealing with the insurance company, bodywork on the car, and so forth). I am thankful we were riding in the Concorde when it happened rather than in our smaller Honda Accord because the Concorde had a much longer back end to absorb the impact; the outcome would have been less favorable had it happened in the Honda. The car seat did a superb job of keeping my toddler in a stationary position and preventing injury. If the kids had not been restrained in their seat belt and car seat, I am convinced they would have gone through the windshield.

❧

Chemical depression, my constant companion since my midtwenties, still plagues me today. It runs in my family (along with alcoholism; they are linked to the same gene). Two of my cousins are also medicated. I have experienced low-grade depression (dysthymia) since childhood, but ongoing verbal abuse in my first marriage triggered my first major episode of depression. I sobbed on the stairway inside my townhouse each day after work for three weeks, and I decided it was time to get help. I went on/off Prozac over the course of several years. After six months on the medication, I decided I did not need it anymore because I felt balanced and felt shame being on it. Then a couple of months later, the sea of depression swallowed me whole again. Back on the medications, I would go until I felt better, off again, then depressed again (for no apparent reason). Without the meds in my system, I felt raw, exposed, and defenseless, just blood and flesh. After a few cycles of this, I made peace with the realization that I needed to stay on the meds for life, as depression was a chronic condition for me. I soon came to find I was in good company. Half the country was on antidepressants, it seemed, and were as crazy as me. It became less of a stigma. I compare my depression to a diabetic needing insulin. My brain serotonin is biologically low, and I need the antidepressants to replenish it.

Thursday, June 7, 2001

I've been dealing with clinical depression for years (it runs in my family) and have been on and off antidepressants during that time. A couple of years ago, my doctor and I decided that I need to be on them all the time. It's a chemical thing I can't help—kind of like a diabetic needing insulin, so I've just accepted it. I went off of it (Prozac) a month before I conceived and definitely struggled with my moods. At thirteen wks. pregnant when they knew there were problems but weren't sure yet what they were, I resumed taking the meds. At sixteen wks., tri 13 was confirmed, and I interrupted at seventeen wks. I normally take 30 mg of Prozac, but a few wks. after my AHC, I was still feeling really depressed, so I upped it to 40 mg. That seemed to do the trick for me. Within a couple of weeks, it was like I was a different person—able to cope much better, and I began seeing the light at the end of the tunnel. What medication do they have you on? Perhaps it's not the right antidepressant for you.

After the birth of my second child, I experienced postpartum depression, and they prescribed Zoloft because they felt it was the safest antidepressant to use while breastfeeding. Well, Zoloft did nothing for me, so I ended up discontinuing nursing and switched back to Prozac. Prozac has worked wonders for me. I call it the miracle medication. It basically transforms me into a fully functioning person and gives me a lot of energy. The glass goes from half empty to half full! That is wrong of your doctor to say he can't help you. You should find another doctor who can experiment with different medications/dosages until he finds what's right for you. It does take a couple of wks. to a month for any antidepressant to get fully into your system and to start noticing results. I have actually been off the Prozac for eight days now cause I'm trying to get pregnant again. I was really scared to go off it, but so far, I'm doing okay. Just trying to get through one day at a time! Please feel free to email me privately any time as I know all about depression. Just try to keep your chin up and know that there will eventually be a light at the end of the tunnel. If I found the light, anyone can, 'cause I was about as depressed as anyone can get after my AHC. Things will get better for you!

❧

A few weeks after the car accident, Mark and I were driving down Evergreen Mills Road, an endless, winding country road with picturesque scenery; we were on our way to a birthday picnic in Leesburg, Virginia, for my friend Meri's daughter. It was going to be a substantial gathering with friends and family.

I stressed at the thought of facing friends who had known Meri's husband, Jack, for many years; they'd grown up together in Solomon's Island, Maryland. My apprehension arose because Cameron, Jack's friend, was carrying a baby with the same due date that Tommy's would have been, June

28, 2001. I hemmed and hawed for a couple of weeks about whether I would be able to handle this. I decided to garner my strength and go.

Halfway to Meri's house, I started trembling and sobbing. My sudden outburst caught my husband off guard, and with a look of bewilderment on his face, he said, "What's wrong with you?!" I told him to turn around and head home as soon as possible. I knew there was no way in hell I was emotionally equipped to deal with her blossoming swell. I was supposed to be sharing in her excitement and showing off my bulging belly as well. Instead, I was a deflated balloon, devoid of life, with a tight-lipped smile plastered across my face like a Botox nightmare.

As Tommy's due date approached, I lay on the ground shackled to the train tracks, knowing the oncoming locomotive was unstoppable. Every milestone date was a challenge, but this first one required expending a Herculean effort to confront.

☙

Multiple pregnancy losses took their toll on my emotions and made it difficult to feel elated for other pregnant women. Even watching a favorite television show risked a stealth missile strike. I posted on the AHC message board, "Well, my due date is fast approaching (June 28), and I am feeling sad. I should be expecting a beautiful baby boy, and instead am feeling emptiness and sadness. I'm hoping that after the date passes, I'll feel some relief. I'm starting to cry as I write this."

☙

I possessed a sixth sense about the troubles to come. Just two months after I terminated my pregnancy, I anticipated problems. I convinced myself that the termination had destroyed my uterine lining. I even emailed a fellow poster on the AHC board when I read in one of her posts that she was a gynecologist, asking her if D&E could cause permanent scarring that could lead to problems conceiving again or carrying a pregnancy; she kindly responded that, while it was possible, it was unlikely. I was desperate for affirmation that I was on the right track.

❧

In the early days following my loss, my emotional wounds still raw, I vowed to never get pregnant again. I somehow mustered the courage six months after my pregnancy was terminated to give this baby-making process another shot. Armed with renewed hope, my overwhelming desire for another child enabled me to gather the courage to try again. I felt strong enough in July 2001 to go for it. When asked by friends what sex child I wanted next time, I replied, "All I want is forty-six chromosomes."

In the thick of my pregnancy quest, I attempted to make light of the situation when I could.

Sunday, August 12, 2001

Thank you so much for your welcomes to me! This is my second month TTC, and my OPK [ovulation predictor kit] line turned dark blue on Saturday morning, so my DH and I had a "fun" weekend (is it fun anymore?! LOL). Keep your fingers crossed for me this month!

❧

I had two avid, steadfast supporters of my cause. My youngest daughter, Ally, and my good friend Meri were my cheerleaders.

Every time a pregnancy test stick would show a second, faint pink line, I could not wait to show Ally and have her double-check to make sure that other line was not a figment of my imagination. She was the sole person in my household who would share my excitement. I know that revealing my pregnancies this early to such a young child did not show the best judgment, but I was desperate for support and shared joy. Mark was not happy each time I would turn up pregnant, and my oldest daughter, Deborah, with typical teenaged enthusiasm, would respond with an "Uh-huh," thinking in her head, "Yeah, right—you're just gonna miscarry again." Ally, her child's mind untainted by realism, would be enthusiastic each time.

Tuesday, August 14, 2001

Just thought I'd share a conversation I had with my three-year-old daughter (Ally) a few minutes ago at lunch. We were talking about her AHC brother, Tommy, who went to heaven, and how that made Mommy sad. She knows I'm trying for another baby. Out of the blue, she says, "The other baby won't go to heaven. I promise the other baby will stay here." Then she said, "Are you excited? Me, too." I can't tell you what her words meant to me. I hope she knows something I don't. They say little children have great insight, so I'm hoping she's right. I'll find out in a few days if I'm pregnant or not this month.

ℰℐ

My husband opposed the idea with vehemence. He was fearful about another chromosomal abnormality occurring and was still not keen on the idea of having a third child in the first place (*what an understatement*). I felt isolated in my quest for another child. Many arguments ensued over this major issue, and I admit that my persistence was selfish. My powerful need to fill the abyss, though, was uncontrollable. My soul was destroyed—a large piece of me died when I lost Tommy, and I knew I must have a baby or I would be forever lost. It became an obsession that took over my life.

My excitement was contagious as the second pink line crept over the test stick like the sun climbing above the horizon at dawn. The first month of trying, and BOOM!—I was pregnant. This was gratifying; I felt optimistic this time around.

Thursday, August 16, 2001

Just wanted to share some good news with you. I took a pregnancy test this morning and I'm pregnant!!! I'm very excited but guarded at the same time. I'll try to enjoy this pregnancy no matter how long it lasts (hopefully, it'll last nine months!). I'll need lots of support, as I'm sure I'll be a basket case!

ℰℐ

A few days after the line on the First Response Pregnancy Test stick turned pink, my children and I went on an overnight visit to see my sister, Karen, who lives a little over an hour away in Stafford, Virginia. Karen has five daughters, and I have always been envious of her king-sized family.

That night as I slept in her daughter Anna's room, I dreamed I woke up and found blood in my underwear, every pregnant woman's nightmare. I was reassured to look down and see stain-free underwear the following morning.

My sister and I went to her neighborhood pool the next day, and she introduced me to some of her friends. With pride, I told one of the women I met that I was expecting. I knew it was early to be making announcements, but I could not contain my joy. Things were looking up for me—life was positive again.

When we returned to Karen's house, I went to the bathroom, and, wouldn't you know, the crotch of my swimming suit was stained with blood. I knew I would no longer be pleasant company. My stomach took a nosedive, and I gathered my kids and started the trek home.

I bought another First Response and performed the test. I noticed the pink line was lighter than it was the last time I tested, indicating without a doubt that the pregnancy hormone human chorionic gonadotropin (hCG) was dropping.

I saw the nurse-midwife at my ob-gyn's office the next day, and she confirmed the pregnancy by performing an internal examination of my cervix. She told me that although bleeding was not a positive sign, she knew of women who bled throughout their entire pregnancies and delivered healthy babies. They drew my blood for a beta hCG test, and the following day, the results indicated that my hCG level was at a level of nine—not high enough to sustain a pregnancy.

Tuesday, August 21, 2001

Not so good news. I'm still spotting, and it's turned to more of a red color. I took another pregnancy test this evening (not the early First Response kind, but the regular kind that you take when you're a day late), and there is no longer any line. I guess this means that I am miscarrying. However, I'm not having any cramping yet. I will call the doctor in the morning. Is it possible to have a definite line on two of the pregnancy tests and then for the line to disappear and your period come later than usual? Is this what happens with a really early miscarriage? Me and my fat mouth told everyone about this pregnancy. I was so excited. You'd think I'd learn. I don't think I can go through this anymore. I may have to call it quits on having another baby. This is just too emotionally wearing for me.

❦

A couple of days later, I bled heavily, and I knew it was over. My hopes were dashed, my already shattered heart now broken in new places. August 2001, a mere two months after the car accident, disaster had reared its gnarly head once more.

Thursday, August 23, 2001

I definitely miscarried. My hCG test results from yesterday just came back, and they were at a 3. Apparently, when they are under 10, you are no longer pregnant and your body has rid itself of the pregnancy. I knew it would be bad news, so I'm not surprised. I am relieved that I won't be needing a D&C [dilation and curettage], though. My doctor told me I'd have to wait two or three cycles before trying again (if I decide to do that). In the meantime, I have an appt. on Sept. 5 with my OB to discuss getting testing to see if I have a progesterone deficiency. Right now, I'm mentally drained from all this loss. Will try really hard not to fall into another depression. The good news is now I can drink Diet Dr Pepper again (my favorite)!! (trying to sound upbeat—LOL). I want to thank everyone for all their responses to my updates and all the loving support I've received. You all are the greatest!!!

✌

I stopped taking antidepressants for my first five pregnancies (my two living children, the AHC, and the first two miscarriages) for fear of contributing to my losses. After my second miscarriage post-termination, I felt like a boxer knocked out in the ring. There was no getting up and fighting anymore without some help.

Friday, August 24, 2001

I'm hoping and praying that everything turns out okay with your pregnancy. It is so hard to go through another possible loss after an AHC. That is good news that the cramping and bleeding have stopped for twenty-four hrs. I wish the best for you. Today, I started taking my Prozac again. I feel myself starting a downward spiral and don't want to go there again. I am emotionally drained and feel like there's a dark cloud over my head. I could barely drag myself out of bed this morning to go to work. I may seriously consider adopting a little baby girl from China. I just don't think I can go through yet another possible loss a third time around. I think it would do me in. I'm sorry for rambling. Just had to get some things off my chest. You are in my thoughts and prayers.

Infertility and multiple pregnancy loss are two factors that rip some of the scab off the shield that the antidepressants provide. I was still depressed during my time of multiple losses but not in an incapacitating manner.

I believe that without antidepressants throughout my ordeal, I never would have survived. It would have been like getting a tooth extracted without Novocain. Several months after I resumed taking Prozac, the depression was milder, my life was functioning close to normal, and I could laugh again. I attribute this to my mother, who was with me every step of the way, my husband's support, a compassionate perinatal loss counselor, internet support bulletin boards, monthly support group meetings, and the glue that held me together: Prozac.

I asked Ally to say a prayer for me at night before she went to bed that I would get another baby. She fulfilled that request for me every single night before she drifted off to sleep. It has been said that God listens with open ears to the prayers of children, so I hung onto the hope that he would hear her.

Meri is a cherished friend who I knew for twenty-four years at the time. Ours is one of those rarely cultivated friendships with staying power, a lifelong bond unscathed by slights or disagreements through thick and thin. She is one of those friends who, if we were to go years without seeing one another, I would still be able to pick up right where we left off.

Ever since my pregnancy termination with Tommy, Meri thought what I needed most to heal was another baby. She provided emotional support throughout the entire ordeal, never failing to tell me she admired my courage and tenacity.

I thought of my aunt Mary and uncle John, from Greensboro, NC, as my telephonic support system during my time of post-AHC guilt. Mary and John had been married forever (almost fifty years) and were an endearing couple, like George Burns and Gracie Allen. John was a retired Episcopalian minister with a wicked sense of humor who could tell a racy joke like no other. He was my father's brother-in-law and best friend and a family patriarch who baptized my twin brothers, Tim and Chris, in the ocean, officiated at my dad's funeral service, assisted at both my wedding and my sister, Karen's, and performed my brother Tim's wedding ceremony. He had nine lives, two of which he'd already used up in a devastating car accident and an aneurysm of the brain, defying all odds.

They knew that I was struggling with self-recrimination after I terminated my pregnancy with Tommy. They rescued me on several occasions via a phone call John would make to check up on me, and Mary would pick up on the other line and join in. They would reassure me that I was not a horrible person and that I did the right thing. These nonjudgmental declarations were comforting coming from an Episcopalian minister and his wife. This helped to ease some of the shame and wrongdoing that plagued me on a regular basis.

I derived healing and encouragement from the words of friends in heartfelt letters. Kayla, a sweetheart of a person whose faith in God I admire, took the time to craft this letter offering spiritual comfort:

Summer of 2001

Suzanne,

I was reading these verses the other day, and you instantly came to my mind. I thought they were extremely encouraging for me, and so I thought I'd share them with you. They're in 2 Corinthians 1:3-5, 8-9:

> *Praise be to the God and Father our Lord Jesus Christ, the Father of compassion and the God of all comfort, who comforts us in all our troubles, so that we can comfort those in any trouble with the comfort we ourselves have received from God. For just as the sufferings of Christ flow over into our lives, so also through Christ our comfort overflows…We were under great pressure, far beyond our ability to endure…But this happened that we might not rely on ourselves but on God…*

I hope you don't feel funny with me sharing these with you—I just thought they might be encouraging for you, too. With everything that you've been through this last year, I know God can use you to help so many others by the comfort that He has for you.

I really admire the way you have chosen to be happy and supportive to all of us around you that have had babies recently and not become bitter. I'm sure that has been, and may still be, very difficult—I know it would be for me. I'll continue to pray for you, Suzanne, and like it says in these verses that He would be a God of comfort and compassion to you.

Kayla

CHAPTER 3

More Bad Luck

Try again. Fail again. Fail better.
~Samuel Beckett

After my first miscarriage in August 2001, I aired my concerns to my ob-gyn; he ordered a test called a sono-hysterogram the following month. The purpose of this test is to check for abnormalities in the uterine cavity. It should be performed after menstrual bleeding has ceased and before ovulation. Sterile fluid is infused into the uterus to open it up and inspect for problems using ultrasound. In my case, they checked for uterine scar tissue or adhesions from my prior C-section and D&E.

There was one hitch. The facility that could schedule me soonest was in Washington, DC, during my husband's work hours. I am well known for my impeccable sense of direction (note my sarcasm). With the confusing one-way streets, odds are I would end up in an unsavory section of town.

I enlisted the help of a former friend, a male colleague who was temporarily between jobs. "Hi, Steve. I have a *big* favor to ask of you." He has a big heart and agreed to assist the damsel in fertility duress. In the city, Steve's SUV was sucked into a traffic circle vortex, which sent us swirling 'round and 'round while he decided where to exit. Little did I know this was just the beginning of my infertility Tilt-a-Whirl.

I took Motrin one hour prior to the sonohysterogram and merely experienced minor discomfort during the procedure. At the conclusion, the doctor said, "Your uterus is the best I've ever seen." *Then why does it continue to fail me?* I thought.

My genetics counselor at GIVF, Heather Donahue, suggested Mark and I undergo blood tests to determine our karyotypes soon after the initial trisomy 13 diagnosis in January 2001. Karyotype testing identifies and evaluates the size, shape, and number of chromosomes in a cell sample. Extra, missing, or abnormal positions of chromosome pieces can be problematic. Her goal was to determine if there were any abnormalities that could have caused trisomy 13 in the fetus, such as one of us carrying a trisomy 13 translocation. A chromosome translocation is a case where a small piece of one chromosome switches places with a small piece of another chromosome.

I was not surprised to discover that I had an inverted chromosome 9, a logical explanation for my peculiarities. I reported the results to Mark: "Now I know why I'm so weird. I have an inverted chromosome 9." After hitting the genetic lottery with the infinitesimal odds of two rare chromosomal problems at once, I was not stunned by this recent finding.

"That explains a lot," he joked.

This is a benign anomaly but an interesting dinner party conversation piece, nonetheless. Neither of us carried the trisomy 13 translocation that could result in future occurrences, useful information should we ever try again.

❧

My friend Lacey, who I cultivated a friendship with via my perinatal loss support group, penned some thoughtful, touching letters following my miscarriages that meant more to me than she would ever imagine.

> *September 1, 2001 (after first miscarriage)*
>
> *Dear Suzanne,*
>
> *It was good to see you at the group on Thursday night. I am so sad to hear about your miscarriage. It must be devastating for you. You were so courageous to try again to get pregnant. I hope in some way that carrying this new baby brought you some joy, even if only briefly. But I can't imagine how hard it must be to go through another loss so soon after losing Tommy. I am so sorry that you have to go through this again.*
>
> *I read your story yesterday. It was beautifully written and heartbreakingly moving. I hope that creating it as well as your lovely poem to Tommy has provided you with some release of your grief and that rereading your story will continue to give you comfort. I hate it that we have all come together because of the tragic loss of our babies, but I am so glad to be getting to know you and Meg, Karen, Reema, and Joan, too. You are in my thoughts and prayers. May you one day recapture your dream.*
>
> *Lacey*

The next tragedy is one that affected us all. After dropping off my daughter Ally at preschool at 9:00 a.m. on a September morning full of promise, I decided to stop by my neighborhood

Food Lion to pick up a few grocery items. While I was in the store parking lot, I listened on the car radio to a broadcast about a plane that had hit the World Trade Center. *Odd,* I thought. *It must have been a small prop plane that somehow veered off course.* I made my purchases, and as I headed out the door, I heard more of the newscast as I walked by a produce truck with its driver zeroed in on the broadcast.

Once home, I turned on the radio to listen to news updates while I unloaded the groceries, and I listened with horror as the news anchor announced that a second plane had collided into the World Trade Center. I thought, *This is no coincidence.* I ran over to the TV and watched the insidious smoke billowing out the side of the building. My heart sank. I called my husband right away and then my neighbor and good friend across the street, Kate. I did not want to be alone at a time like this.

A little while later, reports came through the television of a plane crashing into the Pentagon. At that point, I came to the realization that we were under a full-blown attack. I felt nakedly vulnerable being just forty minutes west of DC. Kate and I called the preschool both of our children attended, and the director informed us it would be best to leave the kids at school in an attempt to keep things as normal as possible.

I remember feeling like a scared four-year-old child, wishing I could just huddle in the corner of my garage and shut out reality. I felt an unease, like a domino about to be toppled over, for about six months following the tragedy. This was the goal the terrorists wanted to achieve.

Tuesday, September 11, 2001
Just wanted to let you know that I'm okay (I live 20 miles west of Washington, DC). I'm just very emotionally shaken up by this horror. I have been very nervous all day. I'm praying for all the people involved in this tragedy.

❧

Another internet message board I visited from time to time was Hygeia. This board was geared toward anyone who lost a pregnancy (by miscarriage as well as pregnancy termination). One of the women I befriended on this site was in a similar situation to mine. She terminated due to Turner syndrome, already had two children, and, like me, was battling with her husband for a third child (she wanted to try again for the third, he didn't). We felt an instant rapport with each another as we were in a unique and similar situation.

My mother, worried sick about me, wished I would give up the pursuit to try again after Tommy. She agonized about my mental state from the loss and, like my husband, feared another anomaly happening in the next pregnancy.

In the wake of 9/11, she advised me that it would be risky to attempt a pregnancy, what with the anthrax and smallpox scares. She would say, "What if you have to be treated for anthrax with Cipro or need to get the smallpox vaccine? It could be dangerous to the baby you'd be carrying." I love my mom to death, but she does tend to be a worrywart. In retrospect, however, I see that she was just trying to protect me, as all mothers protect their children.

Monday, October 22, 2001

I will probably try again anyway. My mom called me the other day, lecturing me that I shouldn't try to get pregnant with all this bioterrorism, etc., going on. She said if smallpox breaks out and I had to get the vaccine, it would hurt the baby, etc. I think I just won't tell her when (if) I get pregnant. She worries about me too much. I don't have the luxury of waiting. I turned thirty-seven today. This stuff could be going on for years…

❧

I commiserated with other women who struggled with infertility issues; as I wrote to a friend, "I can understand what you mean about feeling sad every time someone announces some good news. Although I'm very happy for them, I feel cheated at the same time, and that it will never happen again for me." I was just so sick and tired of going through this cycle of TTC, getting pregnant, losing the baby, having to wait X number of months to try again, and then the stress of TTC yet another time. I wondered how many attempts it would take for just one more healthy baby. It was all so emotionally draining, and I felt like I had aged ten years in the previous twelve months!

❧

Even worse than my playgroup members' pregnancy announcements and baby shower invitations was hanging out with them during their lactation sessions.

Thursday, November 1, 2001

Thanks so much for your responses to my "need advice" post about whether or not I should TTC again given the nasty world events. I am definitely trying again this month (in a few days—I'm on day thirteen of my cycle today and just started doing the OPK this morning)…Yesterday at my three-year-old's playgroup, I was sitting on a couch surrounded in a room by four new mothers nursing their babies. It was like a stake to my heart. At least knowing that I can try again helps to lessen some of that pain. I'm hoping that my third attempt in a row will "take" for a healthy baby. Send me plenty of baby dust!

❧

November 2001 brought more adversity. I had been working for Sprint in telecommunications for fifteen years, the last few years of those part-time. As you know, part-time professional jobs that pay well are like diamonds in the rough—difficult to obtain. My job was to build network tables. I excelled at it and enjoyed the work, not to mention that it helped pay the bills. That day, I received a plaque commemorating my fifteen-year tenure at the company—an irony, I was to find out later.

My shift ended at 11:00 p.m. the night of November 14, and five minutes before it was time to leave, my manager approached and told me he needed to speak to me in his office. This was somewhat unnerving, as there were layoffs taking place in the company. He sat me down and delivered the somber news that I was one of the lucky few who would have to be let go. This news hit me like a punch to the gut and sent me into a tailspin. I started sobbing in his office. I do not reveal my emotions like that on a normal basis, but a dam broke inside me that could not be suppressed. In my cubicle, I packed up my belongings while my manager stood over me like a prison warden guarding a convict. I felt shattered as I drove home, blinded by a deluge of tears spilling down my face.

I woke my husband when I arrived home to share the latest news flash with him. His face dropped as he wondered how we were going to pay our bills.

Thursday, November 15, 2001

Well, I got laid off from my job last night. I'd worked for the company for fifteen yrs. Even though I was just working part-time (twenty hrs. per wk.), we really relied on my income (can't pay the bills w/o it). Luckily, I got a good severance package (thirty wks.) I slept about an hour last night, I was so upset. Yes—we're TTC again. I'll find out if I'm pregnant or not in a few days. If I am, I'd be worried about the emotional outburst I had last night. I guess my fallback plan of adoption is out the window since it costs so much. I'm going to try to find some work I can do from my computer at home (maybe medical transcriptionist— processing medical claims). I worked in telecom at Sprint, and my part-time job paid really well. Will be hard to find another job making that kind of money. I was driving home in tears last night chanting, "Just punch me when I'm down." Sorry for all my complaining. I'm just going through a very rough time right now.

As a side note to add to the joy of November, my sister, Karen, had a biopsy (on the day I got laid off) to check for cervical or uterine cancer, but thankfully (after a worrisome week), it turned out to be negative.

ↈ

Christmas, once my favorite holiday, lost its luster. Thoughts of tinsel, sugar plums, and nutcrackers were replaced with unpleasant memories and regrets.

Saturday, December 8, 2001
I keep thinking that I should have a five-month-old blond baby boy (Tommy, T-13) in my family Christmas photo, or that I should be five months pregnant now with my second failed attempt (the miscarriage)…

ↈ

In my urgent quest to determine the cause of my multiple miscarriages, I researched many different causes/conditions. In the early stages of my detective work, I convinced myself I had a *luteal phase defect* (LPD).

The luteal phase is the part of the monthly cycle from ovulation to the first day of menstruation. This should range from eleven to sixteen days in an optimum scenario to enable the uterine lining to become thick enough to sustain the implantation of an embryo. Anything less than ten days might signal an LPD. A pregnancy cannot be sustained with an LPD because the uterine lining breaks down, bringing on menstrual bleeding and causing an early miscarriage. The number one reason for LPD is low progesterone levels.

Saturday, December 15, 2001

Well, my AF [Aunt Flo/menstrual period] made an early appearance the night before last. This is the second month in a row it came after twenty-seven days (usually, it comes every thirty to thirty-three days). It was our second month of trying. I'm not as depressed as I thought I'd be, but I'm a little concerned about my cycle. Since my M/C in August, I've noticed that my CM [cervical mucus] is slight (even around ovulation time). Also, I've heard that the luteal phase of your cycle (from ovulation to your period) is supposed to be anywhere from eleven to sixteen days. Mine is usually twelve, which is normal. However, this month, my luteal phase was only nine days (I ovulated on day eighteen, per my OPK). Does anyone know much about this? I'm hoping that it was just a one-time occurrence this month. I have been under a lot of stress, so that might be messing with my cycle. I really don't want to be dealing with infertility issues now on top of everything else! Oh well, I'll try to keep my chin up and just keep trying. If anyone knows much about this, any info would be appreciated.

I monitored my cycle for several months (using an OPK) to determine the day of ovulation and found that my luteal phase was just nine days. I was thrilled that I might be "onto something" and started taking vitamin B6 supplements on the advice of a fellow member of my conception issues post-AHC (CI-AHC) message board. This vitamin was claimed to help lengthen the luteal phase. My ob-gyn also prescribed progesterone suppositories for my possible luteal phase defect, to be taken every month after ovulation.

❧

Many screaming matches ensued as I fought for another baby as though my life's blood depended on it, and Mark opposed it.

Monday, December 17, 2001

I can totally relate to your financial situation. I lost my part-time job in telecom (good paying) on Nov. 14. Although I have a good severance package, it seems like all my DH and I do now is fight (about $$ and babies). I have this possible job opportunity lined up for some time in Jan. We've been TTC for two months unsuccessfully now. He just informed me that he thinks we should take a month off TTC until this job is definite. I just went ballistic on him! We had an extremely loud screaming match (actually, I was doing most of the screaming). This is such an extremely touchy subject with me. After losing my AHC baby (Tommy) last January, I am very sensitive to the fact that I NEED to have another baby. He just doesn't understand. Also, I feel like I don't have the luxury of taking a month off. I turned thirty-seven in October. I feel my time ticking away. My DH and I usually get along well, but this whole $$/baby thing is a real sore spot between us. He says I should be happy with the two children I have (which I am) and doesn't understand the dying need I have to have another child. He said, "I've talked to a few people about this, and they don't understand why you don't just give in" (not have another baby). I said, "Well, I'm sure the people that said it haven't lived through an AHC." What a terrible note to end my childbearing years on (AHC). Sorry for rambling…I'm just so upset right *now. It seems like nothing goes right for me anymore (in the last eleven months, I've lost two babies—one AHC and one M/C, we've lost two jobs between us, and I was in a bad car wreck—thankfully, no one was hurt badly). My life just really sucks right now.*

❧

I researched and weighed the pros and cons of being on Prozac during pregnancy and found that the past data did not indicate known birth defects from the medication. A dismal mental state would be more harmful to a future pregnancy. My doctor started me on an antidepressant medication, which began to lift the severity of my depression within a week.

Monday, December 17, 2001

I've done a lot of research on Prozac and pregnancy, and I finally came to the conclusion that I must be on it. It would be more dangerous to the baby for me to be off it than on it (and believe me, I didn't make the decision lightly). After all the crap I've been through this year (in addition to my clinical depression that I have anyway), there's no way I could function w/o it. I've heard that Zoloft is as safe as Prozac during pregnancy and nursing. I got some studies from Eli Lilly (the manufacturer of Prozac) from my doctor, and it showed that the incidence of birth defects is no more than that of the general population not taking the medication. If you feel you clearly need to be on it (if life feels unbearable without it), then I would take it. In my opinion, it would be more detrimental to the rest of your family and your unborn baby to be an emotional wreck all the time (which I am when I'm not on it)! I think there are some other ladies on this list who have been through subsequent pregnancies while remaining on their antidepressant medication. Hope I was of some help here. Oh, and by the way, for my AHC pregnancy and my miscarriage, I was not on the Prozac, and you see how much good that did! If you've read this far, you deserve a gold medal.

Thursday, December 20, 2001

Yesterday was the date last year that I had my sonogram with Tommy at twelve-and-a-half wks. pregnant. I was so excited 'cause they suspected I might be having twins. Instead, they saw one baby with an increased nuchal translucency behind the neck. That was the day my nightmare started. Unfortunately, Christmastime brings back all those awful memories of the dreadful waiting game (I found out my baby had trisomy 13 and an extra marker chromosome on Jan. 12). Christmas will never be the same for me. I'm trying to be hopeful, though, that the new year will bring me some joy (hopefully, a new healthy pregnancy). I'm sorry to be such a downer. Just wanted to share this with some people that I know will understand. Hope everyone has a nice Christmas and your dreams come true.

༄

My mom, however, became a supporter of my cause (I guess when she figured out I was not giving up). She periodically sent me greeting cards containing words of encouragement. One of the cards displayed a big "WOW" across the front with fireworks in the background and "You're doing great!" inscribed on the inside. She added the following personal note:

Dear Suzanne,

I just want you to know how impressed I am by your determination to fulfill your desire of having another child. This is to assure you that I am praying for you and that I'm very proud of you! You are a wonderful mother (and daughter) and you certainly deserve the best!

Lots of love,
Mom

❧

The front of another card featured two birds sitting on a branch in the evening and the moon in the background with the inscription, "As long as you need me…" It was a musical card, and when I opened it, it played "Stand by Me," and it read "… you'll find me right there." She handwrote, "I'm sure everything will work out fine. Lots of love always, Mom."

My mom also assured me that all her friends were praying for me. These were the little boosts I needed to kindle my aspirations.

My mom was a constant source of comfort to me and was always there when I needed her support. In my desperation, I made a comment to her one day that I needed a good luck charm to help break this curse that had been bestowed upon me. She took that request to heart—for Christmas 2001, she gave me a four-leaf clover ornament to hang on my tree. I was grasping at straws at this point, and I hung it on my Christmas tree each year without fail in hopes of the baby-fairy delivering some good fortune.

☙

The year 2001 was one I wanted to banish from my memory. The following year just had to improve, right?

CHAPTER 4

Enough Bad Luck Already!

*I have not failed. I've just found
10,000 ways that won't work.*

~Thomas Edison (attributed)

I hoped the new year (2002) would bring better luck, but it was not in the cards. On January 10, I took an early pregnancy test that indicated I was pregnant again after the third month of trying. I was not optimistic this time.

Sunday, January 13, 2002

I'm glad your surgery went okay. I wish you the best of luck when you start TTC. I took an HPT [home pregnancy test] a couple of days ago, and it was positive. I had blood work taken at my OB last Thursday and should get the results on Monday (for hCG/progesterone levels). Yesterday morning, I had a couple of pink spots in the morning (which had me scared to death all day yesterday). However, I have seen no spotting since. I think it was just implantation spotting (since it was 12 DPO—days past ovulation—about the right time). I'm not even excited, 'cause I'm so afraid something will once again go wrong. Every time I go to the bathroom, I check for blood. I'm afraid I'm going to be a nervous wreck the entire pregnancy. I just hope and pray the third time will be a charm for me. I hope it works out for you next time, too, and that the odds are in our favor this time!

❧

I tried humor to keep myself in a positive frame of mind. In an email to another friend, I wrote, "If AF shows her ugly face this month, I'll just have a quick cry, some chocolate, drink as many Diet Dr Peppers as I want (my favorite!) and have a nice, hot bath with my DH and some champagne."

But, once again, things did not work out as planned.

Tuesday, January 15, 2002

Thank you for your replies to my questions about my beta levels, etc. It looks like I'm getting ready to have an early miscarriage. My beta hCG and progesterone were 8 and 9, respectively, 10 DPO. The results of my test yesterday at 14 DPO were only 13 for hCG and way down to 3.25 for progesterone. I'm having another blood test on Monday to confirm that I've miscarried. The OB said I won't need a D&C because it's so early. I already had a miscarriage last August at only five wks. pregnant, too. My luteal phase on the cycle before I got pregnant this time was only nine days, so my doctor and I suspect I could possibly have a luteal phase defect/progesterone deficiency. He said that after I bleed from this miscarriage (am still only spotting brown), I could try again next month after my period. He will have me take progesterone suppositories every month right after ovulation so that if/when I do get pregnant again, I will have enough progesterone. He said these last two miscarriages could have either been caused by chromosomal defects or *a progesterone deficiency. I opted not to have an endometrial biopsy to check for luteal phase defect and just go on the assumption that I do have one (since taking the progesterone suppositories wouldn't hurt me, anyway). I am very upset and frustrated right now (have had two good cries already) and would adopt in a heartbeat if we had the money. I guess we will just try again next cycle, take progesterone, and hope for the best. I'm about at the end of my rope! I was hoping 2002 would be a better year for me, but I guess not.*

❧

This second miscarriage disturbed me because it happened on January 16, two days before the pivotal date of January 18, the day I terminated my trisomy 13 pregnancy the year before. I always tend to get the blues during the bleak winter months of January and February, a letdown after the festivities of the holidays. *Okay,* I thought, *they say third time's a charm, so maybe the next go-around will work.*

Wednesday, January 23, 2002

I feel like I'm depressing to be around 'cause I am always the one with bad news among my friends. It's getting to be ridiculous (this bad streak of luck I've been having for the last year). I'm putting off TTC again until we go on our trip (we've decided to take a family trip to Aruba to an all-inclusive resort). It's a mental health break for me. My body has been pregnant three times in the last year (AHC and then two M/Cs in a row), my DH lost his job (but now has another), I lost my job, and I got in a car accident w/ my kids (all in the span of this past glorious year). We're going March 25 through April 1, and I can't wait. I'm focusing on losing weight and getting excited about the trip right now. All this baby stuff has taken its toll on me, and I need to think about myself right now. The doc said I could try next cycle, but I'm going to wait till we get back. Don't need to worry about progesterone suppositories/miscarrying while in Aruba.

Are you going to TTC again? I'm going to give it one more shot after the trip and will then call it quits if it fails a fourth time. I'm trying to get used to the idea that I may not have any more kids.

❧

I formed a bad habit of watching *A Baby Story* and *Maternity Ward* on The Learning Channel (TLC) on a regular basis. *A Baby Story* contained fairy-book tales of women through their pregnancies to the blissful birth of their healthy cherubs. This show fueled my baby obsession as well as my grief over not being one of those lucky women. I wallowed in self-pity after each excruciating episode.

Maternity Ward contained episodes of sometimes risky and challenging births, but the end result was always a baby. I have always had a fascination with labor and delivery and, at times, have entertained the thought of becoming a labor and delivery nurse. I thought that perhaps one day when I am a grandmother, I would embark on this career (pardon my digression). Anyway, *Maternity Ward* also stoked my agonizing fire of obsession for a visit from the stork. As I wrote to a friend, "it just depresses me and makes me feel more anxious to have a baby. I don't know why I torture myself that way."

> *Friday, February 1, 2002*
>
> *Just checking in to see how everyone's doing? My spirits have been much better lately. I'm really looking forward to our trip in March. I think I'm finally coming to accept the fact that I *may* not ever have another biological child. It's taken me a long time to get to that point. I'll try again starting in April (taking the progesterone suppositories), and if it doesn't work out a fourth time, I'll move on to adoption. I could get really excited about adopting a baby, too. I talked to my perinatal loss counselor yesterday, and she also counsels people on adoptions. She gave me a lot of good information. I'll get a baby, one way or the other. Maybe it was meant for me to adopt.*

> *Saturday, February 2, 2002*
>
> *I have a question about taking B6 supplements. I've had two early miscarriages since my AHC in Jan. 2001. They both happened around five weeks pregnant. With this last pregnancy, my progesterone was too low with the first blood draw. Also, the period that I had before I got pregnant this last time had a luteal phase of only nine days. My doctor and I suspect a progesterone deficiency, and he will put me on progesterone suppositories when I start trying again (probably in April). I had also heard that taking B6 vitamin supplements can lengthen your luteal phase....*

❧

I invested in a basal thermometer to chart my cycles, as well as the acclaimed book *Taking Charge of Your Fertility* (*TCOYF*), based on a recommendation from a fellow message board member. Armed with these two new tools, I had renewed hope.

Tuesday, February 12, 2002

First of all, I wanted to wish you an early Happy Birthday for Wednesday! I ordered the book TCOYF off Amazon, and it arrived a few days ago. I'm going to buy a basal thermometer and start charting when my period starts (any day now). I know when I ovulated this month (it was obvious by the CM) and today is nine days past ovulation. I'm praying that I can get past ten days before my period starts. I've been taking the B6 for a couple of weeks now. I hope it works to lengthen my luteal phase. TCOYF has a lot of great information, and it'll be interesting charting to learn more about my cycle. I'm not going to TTC again until we get back from Aruba (in April). I want to be able to fully enjoy myself on this vacation.

❧

The judgment a person can unleash on the judged (sometimes inadvertently) can inflict a harsh wound on the target. Sometimes, people do not think before they speak (we are all guilty of it from time to time), and they do not realize the harm their words can inflict.

Thursday, February 21, 2002

There's this lady who used to be in my three-year-old's playgroup. She knows the whole story of my termination due to tri 13 and an extra marker chromosome. A couple of months ago, I was talking to her at the park, and somehow the topic of testing came up—by her (she's my age, thirty-seven, and was a few months pregnant at the time). She said to me, "I'm not getting the AFP or amnio 'cause

*I wouldn't do anything, anyway." Now, whenever I see her at the park, I act cold to her. I can't help it—she just irritates me ever since she said that. She's eight-and-a-half months pregnant right now, and I just saw her at the park again. My three-year-old was acting up, so I went home after only being there twenty minutes. I think the real reason I left was because she was there. I can't believe she would have the nerve to say something like that to me, knowing my situation. What a judgmental b***h! Sorry—I'm just so disgusted!!!!!*

After a couple of months, my luteal phase did increase from eleven to twelve days, much to my excitement. However, my hopes were short-lived when I miscarried several times after treatment with the vitamin supplements and progesterone.

The end of March in 2002 marked a Southern Caribbean getaway with my family for a weeklong escape from reality.

I had traveled to Aruba years before with my ex-husband, Dan, on one of those coveted all-expenses-paid company-sponsored trips, courtesy of Emerson Homes, a luxury home-builder he worked for at the time. I fell in love with this island in the Dutch West Indies, with its rugged beauty in the form of desert-like terrain, rocky cliffs, and an abundance of iguanas. The allure of the native people, with their welcoming and amicable nature, also drew me. I must admit, much of its personal appeal lay in its sheer distance, an exotic fifteen miles, from the South American coastline.

My youngest, Ally, then three-and-a-half years old, had transitioned to the age in which traveling with her could be likened to toting around a ball and chain. Nothing against taking trips with children, but those of you who have vacationed to a romantic destination with a one- to two-year-old can appreciate this analogy.

We enjoyed a refreshing, stress-free family vacation engaging in the four S's: sunning, swimming, shopping, and sightseeing. My favorite part of the trip was renting a Jeep and exploring off the beaten path. The locals dispensed cryptic directions, so navigating from one destination to another was a challenge: "After a sharp turn in the road, you will see a large rock sticking out. Make a right there. Then go until you see a yellow shack. Make third left past the anchor…"

I will never forget gazing down upon a breathtaking scene: a rugged cliff with aquamarine waves hammering against it with an intensity that was intimidating and empowering. I knew then and there that a force beyond my control was at work.

৵৩

After I was laid off from Sprint in November of the previous year, I was elated when I got a call from a former coworker and friend about a part-time job opportunity at a small local technical firm in April 2002. They needed a receptionist with some light technical duties two days per week. After the interview, I was offered the job, which paid well; I thought it was too good to be true.

In record time, I discovered that with a predominance of male coworkers, chauvinism ruled in this office. I was expected to start the pot of coffee first thing every morning and hand deliver the steaming mugs to the "guys" while they held meetings in the conference room. Believe it or not, the CEO instructed me one day to drive his Mercedes SUV to the gas station and "fill 'er up." I drove the fine fifty-thousand-dollar machine like it was made of handblown glass, afraid of wrecking it. Anyone glancing over as they passed me on Route 50 would have been convinced that they saw a small gray head peering over the steering wheel, not that of a vibrant young woman. Alongside the fear was the brief, vicarious thrill of exuding such wealth.

Another job duty of utmost importance included the maintenance of an Excel spreadsheet for the CEO's trophy wife, which included their pricey household treasures and their corresponding monetary values (statues, oil paintings, overpriced andirons, and so forth). The CEO was a commanding yet benevolent eighty-year-old businessman who kept gin stocked in the work freezer along with frozen coffee beans.

I remember one coworker who possessed the personality of a russet potato and always addressed me in a demeaning manner. One day during a business meeting, he shoved the coffee pot in my face and demanded, "We need some more coffee now!" You know I wanted to reply, "You have two hands—make your own damn coffee!" but I restrained myself.

Being a person of reasonable intelligence, I felt degraded by this treatment, and over the year, it began to wear on me. One morning at work, I broke down in tears in the coffee room. I was fulfilling my grandiose duty of grinding the Starbucks coffee beans for the all-important males who awaited their morning brew like vultures. My friend, Dennis, who told me about the job in the first place, was the lucky audience for my outburst since he happened to be in the wrong place at the wrong time. I keep my emotions in check on a normal basis, but I was a clogged pipe that needed release. I erupted into a fountain of tears and blurted out I was depressed because I was preparing to miscarry my $4,000 IVF pregnancy, as I was spotting. He was sympathetic, of course, but I took pity on the poor guy. Here he was, this fifty-three-year-old, twice-divorced, single bachelor with no kids, listening to this hormone-crazed woman bawling and bemoaning her reproductive issues. I'm sure he just wanted to get the hell outta Dodge, and I did not blame him one bit.

☙

A minor blip on the radar screen of my tribulations but troublesome nonetheless, was the breaking of the tip of my ring finger in April 2002. Mark, Ally, and I were in the backyard enjoying a sunny spring day. Our dog, Bear, a large, unruly Samoyed that we adopted from the animal shelter a couple of months earlier, was on a chain; we were waiting to get a fence for the yard.

Ally decided to throw Bear's tennis ball, and he made a mad dash for the sailing object. In the process, he twisted his chain around my feet, which sent me hurtling facedown toward the ground. Using my hands to try to shield my fall, I came facedown with all my weight on my ring finger. As the pain shot through me like a knife, I yelled an obscenity that half the neighborhood heard (unless they were hearing impaired). My dear, sweet husband said, "Aren't you overreacting?"

It was difficult to fall asleep that night with my finger throbbing like a racing heartbeat. It was barely swollen, but I decided I should have a doctor look at it.

An X-ray the following day with an orthopedist revealed a hairline fracture and an accompanying tumor, which the doctor (who looked like Doogie Howser, MD) said appeared to be benign. He recommended surgery to remove the tumor, as it would cause the bone to be weaker in that spot and could be rebroken at any time. The surgery was scheduled for June.

Of course, a small part of me was apprehensive that the tumor was not benign. A biopsy would give me a definitive answer. So I spent the next couple of months with a niggling worry in the back of my mind, as no one likes to hear the dirty word *tumor*.

I realized that sheer determination alone might not result in a biological child, so I began to explore my alternatives, adoption being a major contender. Adoption became like an EpiPen that I carried everywhere in case I experienced anaphylactic shock brought on by loss of hope, which could swell my heart shut at any given time. I maintained a backup plan, something to give me a reason to get out of bed in the mornings. I researched and pursued adoption as fervently as I tried to get and remain pregnant. I needed one more baby in my family, or I would implode. I could not bear to end the childbearing segment of my life on such a dismal note.

I was done trying to conceive on my own by May 2002, after my third miscarriage in less than a year past Tommy's tragedy.

Mark was adopted when he was six months old, so I assumed that he would be agreeable to this alternative; I was wrong. Bottom line, his hesitance boiled down to the money factor, a dominating force in many of his decision-making processes (he is "parting with greenbacks" challenged). But I was as determined as ever to overcome his objections; we would find a way to grow our family one way or another.

ℰↄ

Adoption is an intimidating, lengthy process.

The average cost of a domestic agency adoption is between $20,000 and $45,000. Independent adoptions (where the adoptive parents and birth mother find one another) cost between $15,000 and $40,000. The upside of adopting from the United States is that you can adopt a newborn, you do not have to travel to another country for weeks at a time before you can take your child home, the wait times for the children can be shorter (an average of one to two years), you have access to family medical history, and you maintain an element of control (in the case of open adoption) about whether you are comfortable with the birth mother's situation. The downside is that there is a certain time frame (that differs from state to state) during which the birth mother can change her mind. For a couple who wants a child more than anything, a change of mind would be devastating.

Foreign adoptions cost between $20,000 and $50,000, depending on the country of choice. China, for example, ranges from $27,000 to $37,000 on average. In all countries, most of the waiting children are more than a year old and have minor to severe special needs. The benefits of this choice are that a child is pretty much guaranteed if you meet the criteria and have the funds, there are more children available for adoption than in the United States, and the birth mother cannot come back for the child. The disadvantages are the foreign travel for extended periods, the possibility that the child may have undisclosed disabilities, no knowledge of the birth mother's history (physical, hobbies, and so on), and it entails adopting an older infant, toddler, or child. The costs associated with foreign adoption can also be higher than those for domestic adoption. However, the guarantee of a baby without the chance of him/her being taken away is priceless to a couple in dire emotional need of a child.

Adopting through the US foster care system is the least expensive and quickest alternative, with costs ranging from free to about $2,500 and with about 60 percent of children matched within one year. Older and special needs children (with physical and/or psychological needs) are available through this alternative.

The "Hope for Children Act" enabled a federal tax credit for couples who choose to adopt; in 2021, that was $14,440 per adopted child. It is available for all qualified adoption expenses and can be used for each child adopted, whether through domestic private adoption, public foster care, or international adoption. Topic No. 607 under www.irs.gov called Adoption Credit and Adoption Assistance Programs contains more information on this. Many companies are now offering adoption benefits to employees (paid adoption leave or reimbursement of some adoption expenses). However, the overall costs are still overwhelming.

It is such a shame that in our society, infertile couples must go through such tremendous financial measures that most fertile couples take for granted. Adoption is unattainable for many. My hope is that one day all health insurance companies will cover assisted reproduction costs and that more government assistance will be provided to those adopting. *Hey, I can dream, can't I?*

I navigated various adoption websites, charting out my course for survival. I spent hours on the "Waiting Children" site, which featured photos of some of the children available for adoption in the United States. However, most of these children were older and/or had special needs. I was looking for a child of four years and under, and to be honest, I was afraid that adopting an older child with special needs might be disruptive to my girls. If I did not already have two children, I might have considered it, but I felt this would create more stress on our already stressed-out household. It was heartbreaking to look at those innocent faces, realizing they just yearned for a family of their own.

I once stumbled upon an international adoption website and discovered a photo of a beautiful blonde-haired, blue-eyed, one-year-old Russian baby girl with a cleft palate. I fell in love with her right away and relished the notion of "saving" her. Perhaps by saving her, I could save myself. I dreamed of adopting her, bringing her to the United States, and fixing her palate. I thought of what her life would be like with no parents to raise her and with a defect marring her lovely face that would be so simple to repair.

A couple of months later, I attempted to find her photo again but was unsuccessful, and she was forever lost in the vast maze of the internet. I still think of her from time to time, wondering if a family adopted her, transforming her life.

I put "feelers" out to all my friends, telling them to alert me at once if they knew of any "knocked up" teens or other adoption opportunities.

One day, my former coworker and friend Steve called to tell me about a possible opportunity. A woman he worked with before (who now lived in San Diego) had a teenaged daughter who had recently returned from a mission trip with her church to a Russian orphanage. She wrote me a letter and told me about a five-year-old girl who she met at the orphanage and fell in love with. She included a few photographs she snapped of the little girl and told me that she was super affectionate and liked to give "wet, sloppy kisses."

I tried to get some inside information on how to adopt this child, but the youth leader informed my friend's daughter that this was not permitted. The child's SKU# (a number to ID children waiting to be adopted) would need to be used to track her down, and then I could pursue the appropriate channels. For a couple of months, I attempted to locate her with only her first name and the name of the orphanage. However, I was never able to determine her SKU#. It is sad that she was unattainable, a missed opportunity that she will never be made aware of.

One day, my mom called, bursting with enthusiasm, to relate a phone call she just received from her sister. My aunt Sally lives in Kinston, North Carolina, and visits Atlantic Beach on occasion, which is about one hour away. Sally saw a pregnant teenager on the dock outside a seafood restaurant in Beaufort, North Carolina, telling passersby that she was pregnant and asking if they knew of anyone who would be willing to raise her baby. My aunt then called me to relay the details, and in my naïve desperation, I started getting excited. I instructed her to tell the teen as soon as she could that, yes, I was interested. For about twenty-four hours, I was full of hope.

The next day, Aunt Sally called to break the news that when the uncle of the teen found out, he informed her that *he* would be raising that baby. My hopes were again squelched. This was the most disappointing of all the adoption "misses."

I figured at this point, the best avenue to pursue would be to place advertisements for an open adoption and go through an adoption attorney. However, with my luck, the birth mother would change her mind at the nth hour, and I would be out thousands and thousands of dollars and out of my mind.

℘

On May 10, 2002, we got the call that Aunt Bea, Mark's feisty, hardworking, full-of-life aunt, passed away at the age of sixty-five while mowing her lawn on her riding mower. Her younger son, Shawn, found her lying on the hill in her yard, looking serene.

She was one of my favorite people; her spunk always tickled me. The previous summer, she came for a visit and we went to the South Riding Festival in our neighborhood. She marched right up to the conductor of a kiddie train and tried to help him fix the engine when it broke down. She was a "take charge" kind of person, ready to help.

I experienced her carefree side when, during a trip to Indiana, she took Mark, the kids, and me to the shores of Lake Michigan in Michigan City, Indiana, to feed the seagulls. She stored numerous loaves of stale bread in the trunk of her car. She drove like a bat out of hell.

I regretted that I could not attend the funeral with Mark, but I needed to stay home with the kids; Ally was too young and boisterous to go at the age of three.

I found out I was pregnant yet again (the first month of trying) on Mother's Day, 2002. I took this as an encouraging sign (in conjunction with the "third time's a charm" motto).

Medical staff members should attempt to be as sensitive as possible when dealing with patients who have received a difficult diagnosis. They should be trained to respond with empathy. Their negative responses can make a bad situation worse.

Friday, May 17, 2002

I just got a call from my doctor's office with the results of my beta hCG test, and the number is really low. It was only a nine, which I know isn't good. I'm crying as I write this. The receptionist told me to come in next week for a repeat beta, and she was really short with me when I told her that I've had three losses in a row, and she wasn't compassionate at all. I can't believe how cold some people can be…I can't take this anymore. I'm calling it quits. I'm so sad. I don't know what I'm going to do. I already have chemical depression. This just isn't fair…

Saturday, May 18, 2002

I am pregnant (found out several days ago, but it doesn't look too good). I had my beta hCG drawn last Tuesday and finally got the results yesterday (I had it drawn eleven DPO). My level was only nine, which they said is very low. They told me to have a repeat beta on Monday. I'm sure I'll end up miscarrying again, as my level was eight last time at ten DPO. I was extremely upset yesterday, but am feeling much better today. Whatever happens, happens. I can't control it. I did take another pregnancy test today, and it was darker than yesterday's, but I know I can't hold out hope based on that. I talked to Jamie C. yesterday, and I do have a game plan now. At first, I was going to give up, but I've since decided that if this pregnancy miscarries (most likely will), I'm going to go to an RE [reproductive endocrinologist] at Genetics and IVF Institute who is on my new insurance plan (effective June 14). I'm going to get some immunology testing, etc., to see if they can find a reason for three chemical pregnancies in a row. They have a "repeat miscarriage/implantation issue" group at GIVF. I at least want some answers. Having a game plan at least gives me some hope.

I hope your IUI [intrauterine insemination] works out this month. I'll be keeping my fingers crossed. Please pray that by some miracle, this pregnancy works out for me.

As you can guess, the pregnancy once again crashed minutes after it took off the runway. This third miscarriage crushed my spirits, and I decided to take a breather for several months and emotionally regroup.

Monday, May 20, 2002

I was going to have another Beta done today, but no need. I just did another HPT, and there is no line at all now, so I'm just waiting for the bleeding to start. I was trying to remain positive no matter what happened, but I can't. I'm so sick of tears. It's getting old. After an AHC plus three

M/Cs [miscarriages] in a row, I'm ready to call it quits. I just have to accept the fact that my body can no longer produce children. I don't know where to go from here. My DH is not thrilled with the adoption idea. Says it's too much money and you don't know what you're going to get. I said, "Well, do you think I can do much better? My last baby had six fingers and seven toes (tri 13)." I feel so useless and empty right now. I just want to feel some happiness again, but don't know if I'll ever get over this tragedy (AHC). I thought having a healthy baby after AHC would help me, but it doesn't look like that's going to happen. Sorry for being so negative. I'm removing myself from the SPD (online board for subsequent pregnancy discussion) list and just staying on this list and PREGLOSSAFTER-AHC [pregnancy loss after AHC] until I decide what I'm going to do.

Monday, May 20, 2002

I can totally relate to where you're coming from. I am so very sorry that AF showed up on Friday. Life just seems to punch us in the face when we're already down. I know what you mean about being so done with this pregnancy thing. It's obsessed me for three yrs. now, and I'm tired of it wreaking havoc on my family and marriage. I need to just get on with my life and enjoy what I have (much easier said than done)! I feel like I've aged so much in the last year from all this stress. I really hope I can get my DH on board with me about adoption. Please hang in there, and know that there's someone else who feels the same way you do right now. I'm here if you ever want to talk.

CHAPTER 5

New Challenges

When angry, count four; when very angry, swear.
~MARK TWAIN

I attempted to anesthetize my pain on occasion with alcohol in the evenings. After the temporary amnesia evoked by the mundane drone of necessary daily household tasks wore off and brutal awareness took over, this was the time when my suffering would become more apparent.

I recall one late night when I was chatting online with a deeply troubled young woman from the AHC website. She endured a termination of a deformed baby who was a product of her father's sexual abuse. She was still living in the same house with him, and I was trying to counsel her to leave the house as soon as possible, before he approached her again.

I drank beer during the conversation, not paying attention to how much I'd had, and almost fell out of my office chair. I thought how ironic it was for me, in my current state, to think I was in any position to counsel someone else on their problems.

I also bonded with a newfound friend from New Jersey who I met on the Hygeia website (who also terminated the pregnancy of her third child due to anomalies, was depressed, and her husband did not want to try again for another baby). We were soul mates. On a couple of occasions, we would drink wine and burn up the phone lines, discussing our collective problems.

In addition to alcohol, I fed my depression with food, an abundance of food. During my multiple pregnancy losses, I filled the void with food and lots of it.

My love/hate relationship with food presented a battle I still fight on a daily basis. I love to devour those ten chocolate chip cookies. I hate myself twenty minutes later after the sugar high has worn off, and I beat myself up for the number that will show up on the enemy (scale) the next morning. I classify myself as one who lives to eat, not eats to live. I'm a binge eater/yo-yo dieter with an allergy to exercise—not a good combo.

I am also an emotional eater. Most people do not eat when they are stressed or upset—in an atypical manner, I overeat during difficult times. If I were typical, I would have the figure of Twiggy.

Through all these pregnancy attempts, I added about thirty pounds to my frame that was already twenty pounds more than it should have been. I made several feeble attempts at losing weight, all of which backfired in my state of despair. At one point in May, I posted to the message board, "I've been feeding my depression with ice cream and cookies for about a week now, and it's time I jump back on the diet bandwagon, or I'll weigh 500 lbs. by swimming pool season!" and I emailed a friend, "Yesterday, I celebrated not being pregnant by eating four brownies and [drinking] two Diet Dr Peppers. Aren't I bad?? Perhaps I'll celebrate tonight with something alcoholic…" Levity was the policy of choice at times like this.

May 21, 2002

When you said, "I'd love to at least have a chemical preg-
nancy" [early miscarriage that occurs by the fifth week of
gestation], I had to chuckle. That made me smile. I guess
we have to keep our sense of humor through all this, or
we'll go crazy! Lately, I tell all my friends, "If you know
of any unwed teenagers who are knocked up, send 'em my
way!" Ha ha.

❧

I went on to request a Day 21 progesterone blood test from
my ob-gyn. This test measures progesterone levels around
seven days past ovulation to determine if the levels are high
enough to sustain a potential embryo in the uterine lining.
Much to my dismay, my test results turned out to be normal.

Despite the failures beating me down (one genetic termination and three early miscarriages), I managed to devise a
game plan. In June 2002, I sought the assistance of a reproductive endocrinologist (RE) from Genetics and IVF Institute
in Fairfax, Virginia, for answers after my third miscarriage.
Dr. Allison Brown was part of the recurrent miscarriage and
implantation failure program. I scheduled an appointment for
a consultation on June 26, 2002. I marveled at the fact that
my health insurance covered 100 percent of infertility testing
and up to three IVF and IUI attempts.

Thursday, May 23, 2002

I'm feeling a little better every day. Kind of a roller
coaster, though. After much vacillating, I've made a game
plan. I called Genetics and IVF Institute and had a nice

conversation with the receptionist. She was very profes-sional and compassionate to my situation (of having one AHC followed by three M/Cs in sixteen months)—which is more than I can say for most of the people I've spoken to about this who are related to the health-care field! I've made a consult appt. with a reproductive endocrinologist, Dr. Brown, on June 26. She is also part of the recurrent miscarriage and implantation failure program, which is geared for me. They also do immunological testing, which is good. My insurance will cover 100 percent of these visits after the fifteen-dollar copay. I also found out (much to my disbelief!) that my insurance covers 100 percent of three IVF and three IUI attempts with no copay! Hard to believe! I had to make her repeat it twice to believe it! I don't know if IVF would help in my case (I get pregnant easily—the embryo just doesn't implant properly). Does anyone have any input as to whether they think that IVF might possibly help out in my case (maybe the hormone injections, etc., that they give would help me out)? I figure since my insurance covers so much, I may as well take advantage of this. I know it will be stressful, but I just want some answers. At least it gives me something to hope for while I'm recovering from my latest M/C. Hope everyone's doing okay and have a great Memorial Day weekend!

❧

On the day of the appointment, Mark and I sat in front of Dr. Brown's imposing desk. The woman who faced us: intelligent expert, demi-God, the answer. Her status as savior was born as my eyes perused the canvas of academic accolades decorating her walls. She was my rock and would deliver me from the curse of infertility. She exuded confidence. "What can I do for you? Tell me what's going on," she said.

"I'm thirty-seven years old, I had a trisomy 13 pregnancy termination in January of 2001, and I've had three miscarriages since—all in the last sixteen months," I said. My face radiated desperation. *What magical potions could she pull out of her bag of wizardry to banish my problems?* I thought.

"We'll start with a complete infertility workup. We'll check your hormone levels, egg quality, check your blood for immunological and other issues, check your uterus, and conduct a semen analysis on your husband. I speculate that your issue is old eggs, Lovey."

Not what I want to hear, and why is she calling me Lovey? I thought. Perhaps she was calling me Lovey because she felt sorry for me, a hopeless case; I wondered if this special name was reserved for me, or if she called all her patients that?

Dr. Brown broached the subject of IVF with preimplantation genetic diagnosis (PGD), where the fertilized embryos are biopsied for the major chromosomal abnormalities: trisomy 13 (Patau syndrome), trisomy 18 (Edwards syndrome), Trisomy 21 (Down syndrome), trisomy 16, and trisomy 22 *before* they are implanted into the uterus, which sparked my interest and enthusiasm. After the meeting, I strode out the doors of the facility armed with renewed hope.

❧

The next event in the grab bag of fun was my finger tumor surgery. It occurred on June 27, 2002.

After I was admitted to the hospital for the outpatient surgery, my young doctor (cute as a teddy bear) told me the anesthesiologist would give me something to relax me like a strong margarita. They proceeded to band my arm in a tourniquet-like device that felt like a vice grip, at which point I demanded, "More margarita, please."

The next thing I knew, I was aroused, feeling spacey, from my peaceful slumber. The first question out of my mouth was "Is it cancerous?" Much to my relief, my doctor informed me the tumor was benign.

They sent me home and instructed me to keep my finger dry and in its taped splint for two weeks. It is amazing how limited and handicapped one feels with just a right ring finger out of commission. Even washing my hair was a major undertaking. I now have a greater appreciation for people with handicaps such as a missing limb.

Saturday, June 29, 2002

I'm recovering from my finger surgery (had a tumor removed from my broken right ring finger bone on Thursday, which is benign, thank God!), so this will be brief since I'm hunting and pecking! I also had my consult w/ the RE (Dr. Allison Brown of Genetics & IVF) on Wednesday. Based on my history (AHC due to tri 13 followed by three M/Cs), she speculates that my problem is old eggs. Lovely. I'm currently doing the Clomid challenge test to see if my eggs are shot. I'm on day three of the five-day Clomid regimen. I will have my day ten blood draw on Tues. and will have the results by Wed. I'm scheduled for an HSG [hysterosalpingogram] on Wed., and I'll have a Day 21 progesterone blood draw also. They took my blood on Wed. for the initial FSH [follicle stimulating hormone] reading (the timing was perfect—it was day four of my cycle, and she said it can be taken days three, four, or five), and I think they also took some blood for immunological testing. My DH also has to do a semen analysis to check the quality of his sperm. So, we'll see. She also talked a little about PGD/IVF, which interests me. I just want some answers so I can close this chapter of my life and move on to the next step (adoption) if need be. If my eggs are really bad quality, I guess I'll have no choice. Donor egg is too expensive. I'll keep you posted on the results of my Clomid challenge test.

This ended the "finger saga," but my body wasn't done torturing me yet.

ℰℐ

Another appetizer on the infertility menu was the hysterosalpingogram (HSG), an X-ray of the uterus and fallopian tubes after a dye is injected into the uterus and tubes. In my case, they were looking for problems on the inside of my uterus (such as adhesions or injuries) that would prevent a fertilized egg from implanting properly. The test is performed two to five days after your menstrual period has ended and before ovulation. I was relieved that this test was less uncomfortable than the sonohysterogram I had months earlier.

Wednesday, July 3, 2002

I had my HSG test this morning, and the results were normal. I had very minimal discomfort. It was actually easier for me than the sonohysterogram I had several months ago. The results of my Clomid challenge test are also in. They are also in normal range; the day three reading was 5.7, and the day ten FSH was 6. I had read somewhere, however, that the day ten results should be lower than the day three results, and my day ten reading was slightly higher than day 3. Does anyone know if this is a bad thing? I'm really confused right now. I've had all the infertility tests, and they haven't found any reasons why I've lost four pregnancies in a row. Oh, my DH also still has to do the sperm quality test. I'm going to also ask them to check prolactin levels. They haven't done that yet. I hope this isn't a case of "unexplained infertility," which will be kind of hard to tackle. Any thoughts?

The Clomid challenge test, also known as the clomiphene citrate challenge test, or CCCT, is an anxiety-provoking test whose results can "challenge" your self-esteem; a high mark indicates perceived failure versus the traditional grade of "A" (meaning "old shriveled-up woman status"). The process involves taking a blood test on days three, four, or five of your menstrual cycle for an initial follicle stimulating hormone (FSH) reading. FSH is the hormone that "tells" your ovaries to ovulate. Next, clomiphene citrate (Clomid), a fertility drug, is taken orally from days five through nine of your cycle to tax your ovaries. Then, on cycle day ten, another blood test is administered to obtain a second FSH level. If this level is above ten, it is considered high and can indicate diminished egg quality and quantity.

The day after my second blood draw, I phoned GIVF for

the anticipated news. "Hello. I'm calling to check the results of my second FSH reading on the Clomid challenge test," I said.

"Okay," said the nurse, "let me pull that info for you." A minute crept along like a meandering turtle. "Ma'am, the results of your FSH are a six."

"A *six*?" I asked, seeking affirmation.

"Yes, a six," she said.

Thank God. I'm not ancient just yet. My hopes were again renewed.

However, Dr. Brown later squelched my hopes when she said, "A high FSH value definitely indicates poor egg quality, but a low value does not necessarily indicate good egg quality." Infertility is a cruel adversary.

Tuesday, July 9, 2002

Thanks for your post to me. I have "passed" the egg test (FSH level test—mine was a six), so I don't know what Dr. Brown will suggest to me. I guess it's just a bunch of weird, unexplained miscarriages (which is frustrating). My DH is getting a semen analysis next week, but it will most likely not show anything unusual. I don't know how many times I should try before I give up (after AHC and then three M/Cs in a row). They may just give me the "idiopathic" empirical treatment next time (of baby aspirin and progesterone). Who knows?!! All I know is that I'm very frustrated and beaten down! Good luck with your donor egg cycle. I hope everything goes great!

❧

Mark dove headfirst into the world of command solo performances with the enthusiasm of a third grader getting a tooth filled. Little did he know that the semen analysis was a mere initiation ceremony into the fraternity.

The semen analysis tests for three attributes: sperm count, motility (ability to "swim"), and morphology (percentage of normally shaped sperm). Mark "passed" all except the morphology component. His morphology was 3 percent versus the normal range of 10 to 16 percent, meaning he had a low percentage of normally shaped swimmers. This is supposed to make conception difficult, but I did not have trouble getting pregnant—just *staying* pregnant. Mark took the news with stoicism; it did not seem to challenge his confidence in his manhood. Dr. Brown assured us this did not contribute to my miscarriages, but it could make it harder to get pregnant. That did not make sense to me, as I got pregnant the first or second month just about every time. My frustration escalated.

The situation puzzled my doctor as well, so she recommended an additional detailed semen analysis called a *sperm chromatin structure assay* (SCSA). At the time, this test cost $300 out of pocket; it determines if the man has a higher than normal (greater than 30 percent) amount of sperm with DNA fragmentation. "If your husband's results are higher than this value, it means he could be fertilizing your eggs with damaged sperm, which could be causing the miscarriages due to chromosomal problems. In that case, I'd strongly recommend he have a vasectomy to prevent further miscarriages. If the test yields normal results, you could try a Clomid/IUI cycle with your husband's sperm," said Dr. Brown. This test was loaded with powerful information, the results as daunting as the Clomid challenge test. For Mark, failing the SCSA test was the male equivalent of me failing the Clomid challenge test (and basically achieving instant Gramps status). Ego-affirming, not.

"If you fail the SCSA test, can we use donor sperm?" I asked.

"No way," said Mark, "I won't go *that* far."

Friday, July 26, 2002

I had my second visit with my RE today to go over all the test results. All of my results were normal. My DH's semen analysis showed that he has a low morphology rate. My RE is puzzled, though, because usually, in this case, the couple has trouble conceiving. My DH has gotten me pregnant five times (my living four-year-old daughter, my tri 13 AHC, and three early miscarriages), all on the first, second, or third month. Weird…She recommended that he have a further semen analysis called SCSA [sperm chromatin structure assay], where they test to see if he has a higher than normal (>30 percent) amount of sperm where the DNA is fragmented. If he does, then that means that he could fertilize the egg but with damaged sperm (resulting in trisomies or other chromosomal problems.) If this test comes back normal, she recommended Clomid with IUI using my DH's sperm. If the test comes back abnormal, she said the only option would be donor sperm (which I would be willing to do, but my DH wouldn't). So that's where I am right now in this never-ending saga. All along I thought it was my eggs, but it's not. I'm afraid this is never going to end. My DH took the news pretty well. I'm hoping that if the test results are bad, my DH will be willing to adopt (but he works for AOL and is now worried about layoffs, so I know he wouldn't be willing to shell out the $$$ needed for adoption). The fun just never ends.

❧

Without hope, my spirit would have crashed and burned. I clung to every happy ending shared with me as if it were my life-breath.

Saturday, July 27, 2002
Congratulations on the safe arrival of Joshua. As a fellow tri 13 AHC-er, this gives me hope.

Thursday, August 29, 2002
I have a phone appt. with my RE today at 2:15 p.m. and am very anxious about it. Basically, she's going to give me some test results from a detailed semen analysis on my husband that is going to tell me whether or not we could have another biological child between us. This tests for DNA fragmentation in the sperm that could have caused the trisomy and the miscarriages. If the results are bad, he will have to get a vasectomy. If they're okay, she recommended I try Clomid and IUI next time. I'm at work today and am trying to brace myself for the news. I don't want to cry at work. Send me strength!

The time to receive Mark's verdict was upon us. It was 2:15 p.m., the allotted time, and we sat wide-eyed in front of Dr. Brown's massive desk, bracing ourselves for the news. She opened her thick folder with the poker face typical of a doctor about to deliver a life-changing statement. My mind raced: *If the news is bad, Mark will have to have a vasectomy; will Mark change his mind about using donor sperm? Think positively.*

"I have good news for you. Mark's SCSA test results came back normal. His value is only seven percent," said Dr. Brown. Mark and I exchanged smiling glances.

"Thank God," I said.

"Would you like to go ahead with an IUI cycle next month?" the doctor asked.

"Yes, definitely," I said.

❧

Even when the women from my termination support group got pregnant, shamefully, it upset me. I knew that they deserved their shot at happiness, but I felt left behind, a life raft lost at sea.

Monday, September 16, 2002

I'm feeling kind of down right now. I just found out another friend (who had an AHC) is twenty wks. pregnant with a healthy baby. This will make the second success in my support group (another lady has a three-month-old baby from that group). It's a group that met about a year back, and we still keep in touch. Don't get me wrong—I'm very happy for them and know that they deserve it, but I'm thinking, "When is my turn going to be?" I know I sound like a selfish pig. I just feel like it's never going to happen and that I'm just wasting my time even trying...

❧

However, my hope would rekindle whenever I learned of victories.

Thursday, September 19, 2002
Thanks so much for the encouraging words (about the lady who had multiple M/Cs followed by two live births). A friend of mine also told me that her mother had five M/Cs (I don't know if they were in a row or not) and had eight living children. Stories like that are just about the only thing that gives me hope. Thanks for your encouragement.

❧

My RE, Dr. Allison Brown, said a low sperm morphology would not cause miscarriages. Having no cause for my multiple losses was puzzling. She suggested we try assisted reproduction.

Several months after miscarriage number three, in October 2002, Dr. Brown and I decided the plan of action would be an intrauterine insemination (IUI) cycle with clomiphene citrate (Clomid), a fertility drug that stimulates the ovaries to produce follicle(s) or egg(s). Thirty-six hours prior to the insemination, a human chorionic gonadotropin (hCG) shot is administered to trigger ovulation. At ovulation time, the washed sperm are injected into the uterus with a catheter. The idea was that the (hopefully) multiple eggs produced, coupled with the sperm-washing procedure (which filters out the seminal plasma, the liquid portion of the semen that helps keep the sperm cells viable) would boost my chances of achieving a viable pregnancy (with odds of up to 16 percent).

Prior to the IUI cycle, Mark and I underwent the mandatory precycle blood work to make sure we did not have any issues such as sexually transmitted diseases or hepatitis. The doctor instructed us to have sex every other day, except for the day before the insemination. I was told to start taking prenatal vitamins daily. As the next step, I began taking the Clomid on days five through nine of my menstrual cycle.

Starting on day eleven of my cycle, I began monitoring for ovulation using a home ovulation predictor kit. On day thirteen, I started going into Genetics and IVF Institute (a forty-minute drive) for morning monitoring (blood work and ultrasound) to check the number and size of follicles and the thickness of my uterine lining. When the follicles reached 17–21 mm in size, I was told to give myself the hCG trigger shot, containing a hormone (Ovidrel) that induces ovulation in thirty-six hours.

I produced four follicles, which was considered ideal at my age of thirty-eight years old. However, my uterine lining only measured 4.8 mm in thickness, a little low. Thinning of the uterine lining is sometimes a side effect of the Clomid. The monitoring nurse informed me they like to see the lining measuring 6.0–6.5 mm, but they had seen pregnancies occur with a lining at 5 mm. This was a source of concern for me—I wanted everything to be optimal after all this effort.

Thursday, October 3, 2002

My lining measured back at 4.8 mm this morning. The U/S [ultrasound] tech said it's probably just staying the same. She said that she has seen pregnancies stick with a lining this low. It looks like I'm going to have four mature follicles for the insemination. They measured 20 mm, 19.5 mm, 17 mm, and 15 mm this morning. They took blood and will call back later with the results. I know I'm not surging yet, cause my OPK line was lighter than the reference line this morning. Don't know if they'll want me to trigger ovulation tonight or not. I wish my lining were thicker, but I guess you can't have everything. I'm getting pretty tired from these early morning monitoring visits, waking up at 5:30 a.m., but I guess it's just the price we have to pay. They said I'll have to wait till sixteen days after insemination to take the HPT. Does that seem like a long time to you? I guess it's because the hCG trigger shot can show a false positive if taken too early. That will be an agonizing wait! I'm getting antsy for this to be done with!

❧

The day of the IUI, one-and-a-half hours prior to my insemination, my husband visited the andrology lab to "do his thing," so to speak, into a cup. The room was equipped with a black leather recliner and "men's" magazines. He called me afterward. "I *did* it," he said, relief resounding through the receiver, "and it was so embarrassing handing the cup to the nurse over the counter afterward."

I attempted to make light of it. "Don't worry," I said, "they're used to it." But I was thinking, *It's hard for me to feel sorry for you, buddy. You have the easy part. Try spreading your legs apart regularly for strangers like I have to for my tests.*

After the insemination took place, on October 6, 2002, I was told to take a pregnancy test if I did not get my period by the sixteenth day after the IUI. I did not hold onto much hope for this IUI cycle, as my lining was thin.

Sunday, October 6, 2002

I had my IUI yesterday at noon. It was quick and painless. The woman doing the insemination did say that my hormone levels and the # of mature eggs (four) looked great, but my lining was a problem at only 4.8 mm. She said it probably won't work this month, but that it could. They have seen some pregnancies stick with linings of five. I guess she just wanted to give me the straight facts. I asked her if maybe I have a thin lining anyway (even without the Clomid) that could have caused my three prior miscarriages at five wks. (right around implantation time). She said yes, that this was a possibility. I asked her how we'd work around that next time around. She said I could do injectable fertility drugs and also take estrogen pills to thicken the lining. So, that is my game plan next cycle if this one doesn't work. I don't have my hopes up that this cycle will result in a baby. After a failed Clomid/IUI cycle, is it possible to go straight into another cycle (with injectable fertility drugs) without waiting a cycle? Since time is not exactly on my side (I'll be thirty-eight next month), I want to keep things moving. So far, I'm not too depressed. I don't know how long that will last. I guess I just have to keep myself extremely busy over the next couple of weeks so I don't obsess about something that most likely won't happen this time.

In a nutshell, the Clomid/IUI cycle that followed was a bust because my uterine lining was too thin (either from the Clomid, which can sometimes thin the lining, or because my lining was too thin on its own). Again, no definite answers here.

಄

As expected, I started my period on October 20, and the cycle was a failure.

Monday, October 21, 2002

Just wanted to let you know that my IUI cycle didn't work this month. I got my AF late yesterday. The Clomid thinned my lining too much. I will go on injectable fertility drugs next time. The problem is that I don't have an appt. with my RE for the new treatment plan until Nov. 12 (thus wasting this next cycle) and the following cycle, as we will be in Indiana for Thanksgiving visiting my DH's family during the "insemination time." I know this 'cause my cycles have gotten very regular. So, it looks like we won't be able to resume trying (with help) until January. Maybe we will try on our own in the meantime. I don't know. I'm just very frustrated and tired.

ल

On occasion, I hid my true feelings from Mark to protect myself.

Thursday, October 31, 2002

That's funny what you said about you not wanting your DH to see the full extent of your grief after each disappointment. I feel the same way, and that's the first time I've heard someone else say that. My DH doesn't really want another child, so he is looking for every opportunity to say, "See, we shouldn't be doing this." After my failed IUI this past month, I put on a "who cares" attitude in front of my DH so he wouldn't think I was depressed about it. I feel like this will make him less negative about the whole "ordeal" of trying and trying and trying (and not succeeding).

❧

I met with Dr. Brown on November 12, 2002, and we decided to attempt a more aggressive measure and proceed with an in vitro fertilization (IVF) with the big guns, PGD *and* ICSI [intracytoplasmic sperm injection]. Preimplantation genetic diagnosis (PGD) is a procedure where the resulting fertilized embryos are screened for major chromosomal issues before placing them into the uterus. Intracytoplasmic sperm injection (ICSI) is where the best quality sperm are found under a microscope, and a "good" sperm is directly injected into each egg.

This was necessary to assist with my husband's low sperm morphology. Although my health insurance covered 100 percent of up to three IVF procedures, this added "frill" (PGD) was not covered, resulting in a $4,000 out-of-pocket expense. A big gamble, yes, and believe *me*, I needed to sell my husband on *this* one.

Thursday, November 14, 2002
I had an appt. with my RE on Tuesday to discuss alternate treatment options. We've decided the best route to go is IVF with ICSI and PGD in Jan/Feb time frame. ICSI is where they look for a good sperm and inject it directly into the egg (since my DH has low morphology). PGD stands for preimplantation genetic diagnosis. They basically test the embryos for chromosomal problems before they transfer them back to me. She strongly suggested PGD since I am

a repeat miscarrier (and she believes that they were most likely caused by chromosomal problems). The bad news is that my insurance doesn't cover the PGD portion, which is $4,000. However, it does cover the IVF and ICSI, which cost about $10,000 total. The hard part will be trying to talk my DH into the $4,000 expense. Next cycle (while we're waiting for the possible IVF), she put me on a lower dose of Clomid (50 mg versus 100 mg per day), and we will do another IUI (if we're back from Indiana in time over Thanksgiving). If not, we'll just do the Clomid au natural. She said at my age (thirty-eight), the pregnancy rate with IVF is 10 percent per embryo transferred. Doesn't sound like such good odds when plunking down $4,000, but I guess it's my only chance.

☙

Whenever I would broach a new idea, such as PGD, donor egg, or additional testing not covered by insurance, Mark would balk at first, but, being the big-hearted softie that he is, would soon give in.

Persistence paid off—I convinced Mark to attempt a costly PGD/IVF cycle.

Friday, November 15, 2002
I discussed the PGD/IVF with my DH yesterday at lunch, and he says I can go ahead and do it (even though it costs $4,000 out of pocket). I'm so relieved he's agreed to it. I'm not going to get my hopes up, but I know it's my best shot at getting pregnant (and staying pregnant).

ℰℐ

Two days after Christmas, 2002, my friend Lacey, from my perinatal loss support group, learned of the birth of her adoptive baby girl. The baby was born to a young, unwed woman from Virginia Beach. The law stipulated that Lacey and her husband, Frank, reside in the state of Virginia during the initial week of the adoption. This was an issue since she lived in Washington, DC.

I thought it would be ideal to host my home to Lacey, Frank, and their new baby during this process to save them some money. I also thought it might be cathartic to assist them, focusing on their joy and getting my mind off my own problems. Plus, I was in the middle of some serious adoption considerations, and what more perfect way to get psyched about it.

I will never forget the moment they first stepped out of the car in front of my house with their tiny new bundle and lifted her out of the car, still strapped into her car seat. I was elated and marveled at their good fortune without jealousy, which surprised me. I believe this was a turning point in my healing process; at last, I had relinquished some of my self-imposed mandate of having to bear a biological child to unshackle my chains of despair.

Tuesday, December 31, 2002

Wow! What a roller coaster you've been through the last few days! I have a friend from a termination support group who is forty-four and adopting a baby girl. The birth mother had the baby on Dec. 27, and they are picking up the baby today. Since they live in another state and the baby is being adopted from VA (where I live), VA has a law where they can't leave the state with the baby for several days—I think it's about a week. I've offered to have them come stay with us with the baby. They're arriving today. I'm so excited to see their little girl. She weighed 5 lbs. 13 oz.—a little peanut. I hope your roller coaster ends soon and you have your baby in your arms shortly. I admire your patience and good attitude! Keep us posted.

❧

This newly formed family ended up staying with us for almost three weeks, as they ran into some red tape during the adoption process. It helped me get my mind off my own pain, a positive experience. Lacey wrote to me soon after their stay with us:

January 17, 2003

Suzanne and Mark,

Thanks so much for opening your home to us over the past 2¹/₂ weeks. Your kindness and generosity have been overwhelming, and you have made us feel so at home here. We know it's been disruptive but appreciate your good nature. We are praying for your success with IVF so you can bring a new baby into your lives very soon. It is bittersweet that we share the pain of losing a baby but we are at the same time grateful to have you in our lives. If we can help at all with your journey (including having you stay at our house!), please know we are always there for you.

Love,
Lacey and Frank (& Kendall)

CHAPTER 6

The IVF Party

*Every challenge you encounter in life is a fork in
the road. You have the choice to choose which way to
go—backward, forward, breakdown or breakthrough.*

~Ifeanyi Enoch Onuoha

Thanks to my husband's superb health insurance plan, in vitro fertilization (IVF) was a viable option for us. It allowed us three regular IVF attempts. Many infertile couples are not so fortunate, and I feel for those who cannot afford it. At $10,000 to $15,000 a pop in 2003 (and that was just for a simple IVF procedure without the frills), you needed to be either well-off or willing to go into debt to afford it. It was a huge risk to take, given the chance of success is just 30 percent per attempt in the best of scenarios. When maternal age is approaching forty, the odds drop to 20 percent. There were the "success or money-back guarantee" programs at GIVF Institute, where, for a fixed cost, you could get up to six attempts at IVF for success or your money back. What I later found out was that the up-front cost of this option was *$49,500,* which was way beyond my reach; I would have to explore other avenues. I was in dire need of a solution. Massachusetts was a state that covered 100 percent of IVF costs for a couple, a big incentive to relocate there for those desperate for a child.

Partaking in IVF was like choreographing the dance routines for a Broadway musical. It required extensive studying, intricate planning, painstaking attention to details, and critical timing. The nurses at GIVF handed me a thick, intimidating IVF binder and instructed me to sign up for "Shot Class 101."

Anything to do with medicine has always fascinated me, so I rushed home and dove into the binder, devouring each detail and studying it with the diligence of a recent law school graduate preparing for the bar exam.

"Mark—don't forget about our shot class tonight," I said.

"Oh, shit, that's right."

"Leave work in time to get there by seven."

"Okay, okay." *(Note the enthusiasm.)*

The GIVF nurse held the class in the waiting room at the IVF patient monitoring facility. There were about ten couples in attendance. I scanned their faces to see if they possessed half the anxiety I did. Mark is squeamish about needles, so he was just along for moral support. The thought of sticking myself with a sharp object held about as much appeal as receiving a root canal without Novocain. Being the nerdy student that I have always been, I took copious notes during the presentation and drew elaborate diagrams.

The nurse instructed us on how to prepare the Gonal-F (follitropin alfa, a fertility drug containing follicle stimulating hormone) medication for injection. Since this drug comes in a powder form, it needs to be mixed with a liquid sodium chloride solution before it is administered. She lost me the first time, and I felt like the dim bulb in the back of the classroom whose stomach drops when she realizes she did not "get it" and everyone else did. As the teacher raced onto the next topic, I raised my hand with embarrassment. "Um, could you please go over the Gonal-F mixing part again?" I asked. Heat rose in my cheeks; I felt like the slow kid. The polite and patient nurse explained again, and the light bulb of understanding flickered on inside my skull.

"Okay, who wants to be the first victim?" asked Nurse Ratched. She turned out to be pleasant, but at that moment, she may as well have been that beloved nurse from *One Flew Over the Cuckoo's Nest.* Each attempt at IVF requires roughly 125 injections of fertility drugs, so I had to get over my fears. I opted to be the third victim.

When it was our turn, the nurse led Mark and me into a private examining room and seated us, and I asked, "Where's the fruit?"

"Fruit?" she asked.

"Yes. Pear, apple, *kiwi*?"

"Oh, no. We're not injecting into fruit. You need to practice on the real thing."

Oh, shit.

"But what will I be injecting into myself?" I asked, stalling for time.

"Oh, just some sterile saline."

"Okay, let's get it over with," I said, feigning bravery.

The nurse said my thigh was a good choice. "Swab the area with an alcohol pad and wave it dry so it doesn't sting. Then pinch up the skin and stick the needle straight in, rapid as a dart. Then, slowly depress the plunger and pull out," she said. Usually when they say, "There will just be a little stick," my head is turned the other way in cowardice with breath held. This time, I needed to face the "little stick" head-on. I inhaled a deep breath and proceeded, with success, I might add.

The nurse handed each graduate the parting gift of what

appeared to be a white cake box, full of daunting goodies such as sterile alcohol pads, 19-gauge filter needles, 26-gauge needles (insulin needles), 3-mL syringe with 23-gauge needles, and a 3-mL syringe.

I skipped out of the building like a child who had just mastered blowing a bubble with Bubble Yum. "I did it, Mark, *I did it.*" My accomplishment empowered me.

I determined from my insurance company that the most cost-effective route was to obtain my IVF meds via mail order from Medco Health. The scripts for my drug arsenal were as follows:

Gonal-F 75 IU	30 ampules (doses)	one refill
Repronex	10 doses	one refill
hCG	one 10,000-unit dose	
Tetracycline	28 doses of 250 mg caps	
Prometrium	60 doses of 200 mg tablets, one vaginally three times per day	four refills
Desogen	1 pill orally for 21 days followed by 1 inert pill for 7 days	two refills
Lupron	one 14-day kit	two refills

I cringed at the thought of pumping my body full of all these drugs; I agonized over the possibility that the mail order IVF meds would not arrive in time for my upcoming cycle; I despaired when I found out that my local pharmacy could not fill the order for Prometrium (a progestin) and I would have to travel forty minutes to Leesburg (the closest pharmacy with a compounding lab).

Over the next couple of weeks, UPS packages appeared on my front porch on alternate days; each held a magic potion. With care, I tore into each intimidating carton of medications, brushed aside the packing popcorn and Bubble Wrap, and unveiled the mystery within. The Gonal-F, Repronex, and Lupron arrived enveloped in ice packs. I read the storage instructions with the care of someone with obsessive compulsive disorder (OCD) and noted that the drugs surrounded by ice required refrigeration to maintain their vitality. I perspired at the realization that my fridge would be housing thousands of dollars of medications, and one misguided swipe of my four-year-old daughter's hand (all thumbs and high-spirited, bless her heart) could yield disaster; I envisioned a power outage. I juggled balls of worry with one orb too many.

IVF is an arduous process that I will detail in a later chapter. I will just say there were many tedious, stressful steps involved leading up to the "big day" (transfer of the embryos into me), two of which involved holing up in my friend's bathroom during her Super Bowl party to inject fertility drugs and driving to GIVF in an ice storm for 7:00 a.m. monitoring.

Monday, January 20, 2003

I had my first morning monitoring appt. today. Had to wake up at 5:30 a.m.—ugghhhh. But I guess it's all worth it in the end (hopefully). They gave me the wrong type of syringes for my remaining Lupron injections, so got home at 8:30 a.m. and had to turn around and go back, finally getting home about 10:45 a.m. I keep telling myself it's all for the cause. My ovaries and lining on the ultrasound looked good, so now I'm just waiting for the results of the blood work (should be in later this afternoon). I'm getting into the home stretch (will be starting the Gonal-F and Repronex soon) and am getting anxious. I haven't had any problems giving myself shots so far, so I'm relieved about that! Am a little nervous about the mixing part with the Gonal-F, though. Well, sorry to bore you with all the minor details of my IVF. I wish everyone much luck with their cycles. I think Habie is on a similar cycle schedule that I'm on.

❧

My hopes elevated when the ultrasound showed ideal, thick lining at one of my morning monitoring appointments.

Friday, January 31, 2003

I went in for monitoring this morning, and I have thirteen measurable follicles (and several additional smaller ones)! Also, my uterine lining is measuring at 12 mm. Thank God! I was really worried about my lining (with my prior Clomid/IUI cycle my lining was only 4.8 mm). The U/S technician said that everything looks "normal," a glorious word for me (for once)! They said my hCG shot is going to be on Saturday or Sunday night, so the retrieval will be most likely either Monday or Tuesday of next week. I'm getting pretty excited and am feeling good about things. Wish me luck!!

❧

As I continued with the fertility shots, I produced an optimal number of follicles, and my hormone levels were right on target. I was almost ready to give myself the hCG trigger shot to enhance follicle production. The fertility meds are taxing to your system. They make you feel exhausted and moody.

Saturday, February 1, 2003

I went in for U/S and blood work this morning, and I now have twenty follicles! I was very happy about that. My lining still looks good. They called about 2:00 p.m. with the results of the blood work, and my E2 levels are 2080. They said I'll probably trigger tomorrow night and have the retrieval on Tuesday. I hope they're right, 'cause I only have three nights of fertility meds left. I was hoping that last night was my last night of Gonal-F and Repronex, but oh well. I guess my thighs will have to suffer another night! I find that I'm getting more and more tired as my E2 levels go up. I guess that's normal. I feel like a walking zombie! Will keep you posted. I'm starting to feel hopeful.

❧

The doctor retrieved my eggs on the morning of February 4, and he said it was "a bumper crop." I retired to my bed for several hours, sapped of energy.

Tuesday, February 4, 2003

I had my egg retrieval at ten this morning, and it went very well. They were able to retrieve eighteen eggs. My doctor said that was excellent for an "old lady like myself."

I laughed at that (I'm thirty-eight). I've been taking it easy all day and slept for about five hrs. At first, I wasn't feeling any pain, but since I woke up, have been having some mild cramping (which is to be expected). Nothing I can't deal with. Tomorrow by noon, I get the fertilization results. Hopefully, those will be good since we had ICSI with our IVF. We either have the transfer Friday or Saturday (that is if there are any chromosomally normal embryos). Will keep everyone posted, and thanks to everyone for your replies and support!

∾

I endured the numerous unsolicited comments from friends and family. Well-meaning, empty platitudes can backfire and just be plain irritating. I fought like a cougar against fate.

Wednesday, February 5, 2003

I hate to hear "If it doesn't work, maybe it's just not meant to be." Another personal favorite (not!): "You should just be thankful for the one(s) you already have." I like to hear "I admire your perseverance and courage in trying to reach your goal."

Out of seven embryos that made it to the biopsy stage, only two were normal. On Saturday, February 8, 2003, two embryos with "normal" chromosomes, a boy and a girl, were transferred to my uterus.

Monday, February 10, 2003

I had my transfer on Saturday at 1:30 p.m., and it went well. They found two normal embryos from the chromosomal testing and put in a boy and a girl! It's amazing that I already know the sex of the embryos they put in. I was hoping for three normal embies but am happy with two. Now at least I don't have to worry about triplets. I was on bed rest for two days, which is why I'm just sending this message. My clinic said one day, but I did it for two days as added insurance. My pregnancy test will be on Feb. 18. I'm trying to remain hopeful but realize fully well that this may not work. Please send your prayers my way. I'll need them!!

❧

On Sunday, February 16, I cheated and took an early First Response Pregnancy Test, which showed a positive. I remember sitting on my bathroom floor, raising my hands in the air in thanks to God. There were tears of joy in my eyes as I marveled at my good fortune. I was in high spirits as I pinned many hopes on this pregnancy since chromosomal problems would not figure into this scenario.

It also did not hurt my mood that we were amid the President's Day blizzard here in DC. I adore snow in a childlike manner. I am one of those people who wait up with the kids late at night for the first flakes to hit and get mad when the totals do not measure up to the predictions. With ten inches already on the ground, twenty-four inches in all were predicted by Monday.

Sunday, February 16, 2003

I'm so thrilled for you! You must be ecstatic! You so deserved this news. Guess what?! I have some news of my own. I couldn't stand the suspense anymore, so I took an HPT about an hour ago, and there was a second pink line (rather dark) after about thirty-eight seconds. I'm in disbelief right now! They say the hCG is out of your system (from the trigger shot) after twelve days, and today would be fourteen days since my hCG shot, so it looks like it's probably an accurate result. I won't get too excited till my beta hCG blood test on Tuesday but must admit I'm very hopeful. I've already figured out that the due date would be Oct. 22, my birthday. I'll try not to read too much into that. We're having a blizzard right now. We live in the Washington, DC area and already have about ten inches of snow on the ground. We're supposed to have twenty-four-plus inches when it's done (by noon Monday). I love snow, so this is a pretty happy day for me!

Congratulations to you!!

✌

On Monday, February 17, 2003, we got an unexpected call. My mother-in-law, Doris, had passed away from a probable heart attack. An ever-faithful employee, she did not show up for work that day, and a coworker and a policeman found her deceased on her kitchen floor. The faucet in her kitchen sink was still running when they found her, so she was doing dishes when she passed. I was suspicious when my voicemail message was not returned the prior Saturday morning telling her about my positive pregnancy test with the two embryos. She was always prompt about calling back.

I had waded through the snow earlier that morning with delicate care (so as not to disturb the "twins"), happy with the success. This news brought my euphoria to an abrupt halt.

Mark and I arranged child care (my mother) in short order, made flight plans, funeral arrangements, packed, and so on. We hired a service to clean the wall of snow off our driveway, something out of character for my frugal husband.

We left on February 19 in the aftermath of the blizzard. We arrived at satellite parking at Dulles International Airport to be greeted with no available parking (many spots were covered with mounds of snow). To avoid missing our flight, we accelerated our car up onto a mountainous pile of snow the size of Mount Everest; in effect, to "create" a parking spot in an unshoveled space. A stressful time indeed.

The wake was Friday evening and the funeral on Saturday. The spotting began at the wake, and the bleeding started at the funeral. Let me just tell you that losing a $4,000 pregnancy while you are looking at your deceased mother-in-law in her casket is about as bad as it gets.

I made an appointment at the local doctor's office in Walkerton, Indiana, after the funeral to check my blood hCG levels, hoping to God they were high enough to indicate a salvageable pregnancy, yet knowing in my heart it would be a complete waste of time. The hCG level turned out to be sixteen when it should have been in the 100s by then. This confirmed my worst fears.

Mark and I spent the next day-and-a-half sorting through the myriad of paperwork, years of accumulated history, in my mother-in-law's house. This served as a distraction to get my mind off my own inner turmoil.

Doris died at age sixty-four, a mere three months prior

to her well-deserved retirement. This was an injustice to this woman who had worked so hard all her life, first as a home daycare provider and later as an aide in the local nursing home. She had a significant impact on my life. I admired her work ethic, spirituality, ability to appreciate the simple things in life, and loyalty.

When I read her journal entries after her death, I learned about her strong faith in God and the hopes she had for her children. One of the entries read, "I wish and pray that Mark meets a nice woman to share his life with," dated July 1993, three months before Mark and I had our first date.

Doris took unadulterated pleasure in the simple things, like noticing a bluebird in a tree, going out for coffee with a friend, or taking a walk down the beach.

Her youngest son, Jim, battled severe alcoholism, and she stood by his side during that time like a guard and held his hand through the ugly times. She possessed unconditional love for him and offered unwavering support.

She had an uncanny devotion to her older sister and best friend, Bernice (Aunt Bea), who passed away only nine months before her. She was brokenhearted after Bea's death; she lost some of her zest for life at that point.

A heartfelt hug at the graveside and many more to follow came from Doris's best friend, Julie, who knew about the miscarriage in progress. I believe God sent her to me. She was an angel personified and had a profoundly comforting effect on me. She is that one-of-a-kind person who makes you feel like you've known her all your life when you first meet her. Ever since, I have kept in touch with her on a regular basis and still feel a close bond.

This fourth miscarriage was like a cannon exploding on my hope—it blew the theory of age-related chromosomal problems causing my losses. Still no answers. I started to believe my body was rejecting these pregnancies with no explanation, that staying pregnant for nine months would be an impossibility.

February 25, 2003

I have been out of commission for a while because my mother-in-law passed away suddenly, and we had to make the trip to Indiana for the funeral. We left last Wed. and just got back. Sun. evening. I miscarried while at the funeral. Two embryos with perfect chromosomes transferred, and still yet another chemical pregnancy. This makes four chemical pregnancies since my AHC. This blows their theory of the chemical pregnancies being due to chromosome problems. They've tested me for everything (blood immunity issues, too) and have turned up nothing. For some unknown reason, my body is rejecting every embryo at five weeks pregnant (since my AHC). Although two HSG tests and a sonohysterogram have turned up no scarring, I believe my uterine environment has been ruined since the AHC. I am officially giving up on trying for any more biological children. Trying to cope, but finding it very hard.

Following this fourth, most devastating miscarriage, the overwhelming advocacy from family and friends helped carry me through these persistent struggles. The saying "It takes a village" rang true in my case.

February 28, 2003

Dear Mark and Suzanne,

We are writing to express our sorrow upon learning of the death of Mark's mother. We understand that she died unexpectedly and that it came as quite a shock. Your family has suffered quite a few losses over the past two years, and we know that you had been hopeful of a brighter 2003. We can imagine Suzanne's recent miscarriage has only enhanced your pain and grief.

It all seems so unfair, and it truly is. You are such kind, caring, and loving people, and you deserve joy in your lives, not so much sadness. When we stayed with you in January, it was so heartrending to see your family, your togetherness, your love. Although you have suffered much more than anyone should ever have to, you are also blessed with a wonderful family. May your love for one another sustain and support you through all your pain.

Love,
Lacey and Frank

∾

In March 2003, one month after the coffee room incident at my part-time job at a small local technical firm, I quit. After I deposited a $23,000 check into the company bank account during my lunch break, I never returned. I notified them when I got home that I would not be coming back, ever. It was not my normal modus operandi to leave an employer high and dry without a two-week notice, but I had reached a breaking point (and was also pumped full of the synthetic hormones Lupron, Gonal-F, and Repronex) and knew what I must do to preserve what shred of sanity I still possessed. In retrospect, I believe this decision was spot-on and precisely the respite I needed.

Monday, March 10, 2003

I'm terribly sorry to hear about your second AHC. That is something no one should have to endure once, much less twice. I can feel the pain in your message. We have similar situations in that my DH didn't want another child, either (we have two girls now, ages four and fourteen). My AHC was in Jan. 2001 due to trisomy 13 (a boy), and since then, I've had four early miscarriages (all at five wks.). My latest miscarriage was from IVF with PGD, where they biopsy the embryos for chromosomal problems before they put them into you. They put in a boy and a girl embryo, but it didn't work out. So, I am out $4,000 and no baby.... I've decided to quit trying but am secretly hoping for an accident. However, an accident scares me because I think another chromosome problem could happen again. I'm trying to move on with my life right now, but it's very hard. People say I should be thankful for the two I have, which I am, but that doesn't get rid of the pain. I was working part-time (two days a week) making good money, but I quit last week so I can have more time at home with the two I do have (and there were issues at work, and I didn't need the added stress of that). We will be really tight for money, but I felt like I had to do it (I felt like I was losing it). I am also thirty-eight (turned thirty-eight in October) and realize this is probably the end of the line. It's very hard to accept, though. I'm sorry for rambling on about myself. If you ever need to talk, I can give you my phone number.

❧

Several months earlier, I'd had a phone call one somber evening from my cousin Lexie, a comical person who has always been able to elicit laughter from me. I have felt a rapport with her since childhood when our families rented beach houses together in the summers. I have colorful memories of meeting boys, strolling down the beach to the arcade, and laying out with suntan oil (sans sunscreen) to see who could get the best tan (or sunburn). This, of course, was in the era before skin cancer awareness.

Lexie mentioned a Southern Caribbean Carnival cruise her family would take for a week over Easter (2003), and how wonderful it would be if our family could join them. I told her it sounded amazing, trying to convince myself for about twenty minutes that it might happen. I knew that my husband, however, would never agree to it due to the expense and the last-minute notice.

That night I slid it past him with a strategy: after he drank a couple of beers, when his defenses were down and his spirits up. He said he would think about it (a small miracle), and within a few days, I somehow convinced him to go. I must admit, I played the sympathy card like a fine-tuned fiddle. There are some advantages to having an incessant run of bad luck.

The cruise originated and ended in San Juan and included visits to St. Thomas, St. John, Martinique, Barbados, and Aruba. This was our first cruise, so we visualized it like a fantasy.

A couple of days before our departure, to keep the flame of bad karma alive, our daughter, Ally, four years old at the time, came down with a virus with a high fever. Right as our plane was touching down in San Juan, Ally threw up into my husband's hand; he did not have time to grab an airsickness bag. "Welcome to San Juan," Mark enthused sardonically as we landed.

With the illness, the much-coveted Kids Club (a parents' answer to prayer) was out of the question, so we got to watch with envy as my cousin's youngest daughter, Stacy, eagerly joined the other kids for hours of activities while her mom and dad lounged by the pool. However, with the miracle of Children's Motrin, we were able to experience periods of fever-free bliss here and there.

During the periods when Ally felt better, we enjoyed snorkeling in St. Thomas and shopping and a boating trip in Barbados. We decided to hang back on the ship for the Martinique stop. Our adventures concluded with a memorable stop in Aruba.

Our Aruba excursion, our most coveted destination, began as a bust. The weather was cloudy and overcast as we rented our two Jeeps to set out on our explorations. All of a sudden, a downpour started, much to our chagrin as we were in open-top vehicles. Our first reaction was "Oh, shit!" but soon we realized that once you are soaking wet, you can't get much wetter, so why not just go with it? We tried to take shelter under a divi-divi tree, which was pointless and hysterical. Then we spotted an abandoned hut with a covered porch, so we sought shelter there. My cousin's eldest son, Jake, then fifteen and quite the comedian, proceeded to take his sopping beach towel and lay it on the road, lie down on it, and announce, "I'm just gonna catch some rays" while the rain pelted him. We all erupted in laughter, the hysterical, cleansing type that comes in the middle of the night when you suddenly wake up giddy with your spouse and find something hilarious that actually isn't so funny. Then, we were caught off guard as the front door creaked open and a native woman and her kids appeared on the porch, staring at us in bewilderment. All I could manage was a *"Lo siento,"* Spanish for "I'm sorry," as the local dialect, Papiamento, is a Creole language blend of Spanish, Dutch, African, Portuguese, French, English, and Arawak Indian. Our motley crew then proceeded to flee the scene like a racing bull rampage, roaring with laughter.

The climate in Aruba is temperate, with an annual average temperature of mideighties and an average rainfall of around an hour's duration (in total). We managed to get that annual hour of rain in our four-hour stay as luck would have it. The deluge did abate in time for us to tour the Natural Bridge, a natural rock formation, and Baby Beach, with shallow, turquoise-colored water so translucent the bottom can be seen for a great distance.

It's ironic that our Jeep jaunt turned out to be the most rewarding and comical part of the entire trip to Aruba, etching a memory that will remain in our minds for years to come.

Don't get the wrong idea about Caribbean vacations as therapy. I do not imply that you must spend a great deal of money by traveling to exotic ports to heal. The point is to engage in an activity that you relish and gets your mind off the ever-looming baby quest, a time to regroup. Do whatever (legal, nondestructive) thing possible to buoy your spirits during this stressful, depressing time, whether that's diving into a gargantuan hot fudge sundae with mountains of whipped cream and a maraschino cherry on top, a drive in the country, or a beach trip. Well, the sundae might be destructive to your diet, but if you don't tell, I won't.

ᔕᔕ

After my fourth miscarriage, I decided I no longer needed birth control. I figured, *What the hell*. Birth control was for people who wanted to prevent pregnancy, and my body was its own personal baby repellent.

Well, wouldn't you know, I got pregnant again for about five minutes, and, big surprise, the flight never gained the momentum needed to leave the runway. My self-confidence eroded at this point. The date of miscarriage number five, the latest and greatest, was May 10, 2003. The possibility of a baby dangled before me like an unattainable prize. The prospect was carried out to sea in an unrelenting riptide, forever lost. After all this, I felt like I'd traversed the nine circles of hell in *Dante's Inferno*.

Sunday, May 18, 2003

Sorry I've been so quiet lately and unable to offer much support. I had another miscarriage last week (another chemical PG at five wks. along). We weren't even trying and got pregnant. I knew all along I'd miscarry, though. That'll now make five chemical pregnancies in a row since my AHC a little over two yrs. ago. I've had many tests by my RE, and they can't find a reason. I had an appt. with my RE last week, and she said she believes it's been chromo-some problems every time (even with the miscarriage from my PGD/IVF in Feb.—she said that since the PGD only checks for the top eight chromosome problems, that my two embryos failed to implant due to chromo problems). I find all that very hard to believe. I mean, I'm only thirty-eight yrs. old. I could understand if I was fifty-two, but it's hard to believe I've had pregnancies with chromosome problems the last six PGs in a row!

❦

I heard about color Doppler ultrasound studies to evaluate blood flow to the lining of the uterus from the CI-AHC online support board a couple of months earlier. To prepare for this test, you must use ovulation predictor kits just prior to ovulation, and when the line turns dark blue (indicating impending ovulation), it is time for the studies. This procedure can determine if the uterine lining is adequate (has enough blood flow) for implantation to occur. A computer converts the Doppler sounds into colors that show the speed and direction of blood flow through the uterine blood vessels.

Before the test, Dr. Brown told me that if my uterine lining was found to be thin, it could be treated with injectable fertility drugs and estrogen pills.

Sunday, May 18, 2003

I've requested some color Doppler ultrasound studies on my uterine lining this month to see if perhaps my lining is too thin to support a pregnancy on a natural cycle. My lining was nice and thick for my PGD/IVF cycle, but I was pumped full of fertility drugs that thickened it. Then, next month, I've requested an endometrial biopsy to check for hormonal problems (luteal phase defect) that could be causing the early M/Cs. I've had the day 21 progesterone test, which came back normal, but I've heard that the true way to find out if you have this issue or not is to have the endometrial biopsy. I've heard it's really painful, but hey, I've gone through so much pain already; what's a little more? Dr. Brown also said if these tests are inconclusive, she could refer me to the expert in the country for recurrent pregnancy loss, a Dr. Joe Hamm in Boston, MA…

❦

Always having a plan, with accompanying backup plans, buoyed my spirits. A scheme represented faith and forward motion. Without one, I was sure to face certain demise. I always conjured up new ideas, from adoption to further infertility tests to donor egg to donor sperm to you name it. I was not going to settle for a dead end; the road branched out ahead of me in different directions, each forming the possible pathway to a child.

Saturday, May 24, 2003

As far as what I feel like I can handle, each time I have a miscarriage, the week of the M/C, I'm ready to call it quits and never try again. Then, after I start feeling a little stronger mentally (and after the hormones clear my system), I start thinking about Plan B, although at this point, I feel like I'm onto Plan Q already! Right now, my RE has me doing ovulation predictor kits, and when the line turns dark blue, I'm to come in for some color Doppler ultrasound scans of my uterine lining (to see how my lining looks on a natural cycle without fertility drugs). Then, I'm going to have a uterine biopsy next month. It's hard to get motivated to do all this, though, 'cause I feel like I'm just grasping at straws at this point. I wish I knew for sure that it was my eggs that were the problem, 'cause then I'd move on to donor egg, but before I would make that investment, I'd want to make sure that it wasn't my uterine environment that was causing all these early losses. I never in a million years thought that after my AHC, I would face infertility. I thought that all I'd have to face would be anxieties about another chromosome problem in a subsequent PG, but I can't even get my pregnancies off the runway, so to speak. What a big, frustrating mess! What are your plans at this point?

∾

I lived with a veil of tears just behind my eyes, ready to spill at any given moment. I convinced myself the gray cloud that had followed me for years was God's punishment for my abortion. I wore my guilt like a tattoo: permanent, never fading.

Monday, June 9, 2003

I find myself very burned out these days and have a constant feeling of general mild depression (even though I'm on antidepressants). I ask myself when (and if) the pain will ever end. It's very hard for me to get myself out of bed in the mornings and I've gained about 30 lbs. out of frustration.

CHAPTER 7

Losing It

The great art of life is sensation;
to feel that we exist, even in pain.
~Lord Byron

In June 2003, I went on a four-day girls' getaway to Dewey Beach, Delaware, with my good friends Meri, Tanya, and Candace. This was to be a carefree time of fun, sun, and relaxation.

Our second evening there, we were sitting in the hotel room having a couple of glasses of wine, sharing "girl talk,"—you know, the usual midbuzz topics that universally arise when a group of women is drinking: men-bashing and sex. After a while, I suggested that we "go out on the town."

We went out to dinner at one of the local dives and then took a shuttle bus (at my insistence) to a beachy bar that college-aged kids frequented. The place was packed, and we geezers looked out of place, like twenty-something wannabes. Meri and Tanya did not drink much, but Candace was my "party buddy" and continued drinking with me. After we danced with one another for a while (I have "white man's disease," no rhythm on the dance floor, so I am sure it provided plenty of comedic entertainment for the hipper crowd), my friends were ready to go, much to my disappointment.

On the shuttle bus on the way back to our hotel, my outspoken, drunken mouth flapped away. I shouted "Yo!" to a young guy sitting right across from me, and he did not much care for it. My friends were afraid I (this suburban housewife) was going to instigate a brawl. I averted this disaster when I listened to the wise advice of my gal pals and shut the hell up.

After the bus deposited us in front of our hotel, I commissioned Candace, my partner in crime, to have another drink with me in a tavern with a boar's head displayed on the sign out front (I do not know why I recall this detail). After our drink (or was it drinks?), we lumbered over to a bench outside and planted ourselves there for a while.

As always, my depression over the baby surfaced during my drunkenness, and I "went there" and told Candace how despondent I was over losing Tommy and my many miscarriages that followed. She put her arms around me and comforted me.

When we decided to retire for the night, we realized we had no idea how to get back to our hotel. Now Candace and I are both known for our pathetic senses of direction, but let's face it—it was the copious amounts of alcohol ingested that played the main part in this. I mean, we were only a block or two away.

Meri and Tanya sent out a search party for us and found us stranded on the bench, with me a mascara-smeared, raccoon-like mess.

That night (and every night of our stay), Meri told me that I had nightmares and cried out in my sleep in distress. The next morning, I stayed in the room and nursed an ample hangover from the previous night's festivities while my friends enjoyed themselves soaking up the sun on the beach.

My losses depressed and haunted me, and when we returned home, Meri told my husband that she was rather worried about me.

❧

My self-torture continued after I got home, and in my despondency, I somehow coerced my husband into something he adamantly opposed: He finally agreed to consider adoption as a future alternative. A miracle indeed.

Monday, June 9, 2003

I am ready to call it quits on having another biological child and want to adopt. However, my husband is not on board with me either on adoption. We had a heart-to-heart the other night, and he agreed to reconsider the adoption thing next April (when he finds out if his job at AOL is stable—they're working on a contract right now that is supposed to end at that time). However, I know it's something he doesn't want to do but is only trying to appease me because I'm devastated.

❧

The final blow came in July 2003, when one of my best friends, Meri, delivered the news of her pregnancy. It felt like a fatal stab to the gut. This tore away the final sinew that held my heart in its chest.

The numerous pregnancy announcements of my friends over the past couple of years beat me down, and Meri would always say, "You don't have to worry about me getting pregnant—we're definitely done." Her husband had undergone a vasectomy, which I would later discover did not "take." I always thought if she were to become pregnant, I would be devastated.

"It was an accident," she said. She kept the news to herself for weeks—she was afraid of what it would do to me. Right after she found out she was pregnant, she called my husband at work to ask for his advice. She told Mark she did not have the heart to tell me and did not know what to do. Mark agreed it would shatter me.

She eventually told me, figuring it would soon be obvious. I was not mad—I was crushed; I knew I had to keep a distance for a while for self-preservation. With this news came the culmination of my collective loss and heartache over the last couple of years.

Friday, July 25, 2003

I'm not having a good day today at all. I got some distressing news from my good friend that she is pregnant (by accident—her DH had a vasectomy a while back that didn't "take" all the way). She has two kids, and they were not planning on having any more. I always used to joke with her and say, "Please don't get pregnant by accident; that will be the thing to send me over the edge," and now it has happened. I'm ashamed of myself for feeling so upset by this, and I wish her the best, but this news feels like a knife that's already in my heart being twisted even deeper. And if that's not bad enough, I was just talking to a neighbor in the street who lives diagonally from me, and I had noticed that she'd been putting on a little weight lately, and she *has a little mound on her stomach (of course, I didn't say anything!). I believe she's pregnant, too. I am feeling very sorry for myself today and just feel like screaming! I was supposed to go to a scrapbooking party with my good friend (who just told me she's pregnant), and I don't know if I can be around her just yet—I need to digest this news. Oh, she also told me she's known for three wks. and told all these other people, but was afraid to tell me. She even called my DH a couple of weeks ago and told him and asked him how she should handle this. Of course I'm not angry with her, but I don't know how I'm going to be around her as her belly grows. I feel so green with envy. I called my DH at work and told him I now know about Meri (my friend) and that I have to resolve this situation of having another baby quickly (I need to start the adoption process soon) or I will go crazy. Of course, he doesn't want to spend the $$, and he's worried about his job at AOL (there are supposed to be layoffs in his group over the next several months). This is causing a huge strain on our relationship....*

෴

In the summer of 2003, several months after my devastating miscarriage of the IVF/PGD pregnancy, I decided to acquire a new addition to our family, a kitten. This would be just the catharsis I needed to help fill a void in my life and would be a diversion on which to focus my maternal instincts.

One Saturday morning, I made it my mission to buy a new cat by day's end. When I set my mind to something, there is generally no stopping me. I scoured the classifieds for kittens. I was elated to find an ad for a litter of Himalayan kittens in Sperryville, Virginia. Although pricey at $250 each, I was set on this breed, as I had owned one before, and they are gorgeous and congenial.

As anyone who knows me well is aware, driving is not one of my preferred activities, especially to novel, faraway destinations. My sense of direction leaves something to be desired. On this day, however, I was up for an escapade, in part to get my mind off my troubling thoughts.

I set off on the journey with my two daughters and Liza, Deborah's cousin, in tow. The final leg of the one-and-a-half-hour car trip involved meandering down a never-ending dirt trail with cows strewn in the middle of the road. We went off the beaten path and landed in the boonies. The eventual destination was a minute, ramshackle house that was a culture shock for the kids—one that would make them appreciate their privilege.

A stout woman and her red-headed daughter, both amiable, greeted us at the front door. They led us upstairs and down a narrow hallway to the kittens' room, where the air hung thick like brocade curtains and the heat sweltered. I wondered how the kittens could survive in these desert-like conditions.

Seven adorable fur balls scurried around the room, winning our hearts, and we had the arduous task of selecting just one. I asked the teenager which one she favored, and she pointed to a male who she said possessed a remarkable personality. I selected him based on her assessment. I almost felt guilty choosing him, as I would be taking the apple of her eye.

The breeder stepped in and said it would be ideal if I could take two siblings to keep them together (for a bargain of $300 for the two). Being the sucker that I am, I of course agreed to this. I chose a female kitten with a sweet and docile personality. After we paid the breeder and she gave us the papers stating they were pure, we set off on our trek home.

My hubby was disgusted to arrive home from work to find not one but two kittens to greet him. However, they soon grew on him.

I took much pleasure and contentment from these cats, who I named Max and Mia, and transferred some of my pent-up maternal energies toward these babies. Arriving on the heels of the loss of my girl and boy embryos from the latest miscarriage, I liked to believe they were a consolation prize that replaced the twins in some way. They mitigated some of the demons that were suffocating my well-being and gave me the energy to motor ahead.

I resorted to having the gold standard for diagnosing luteal phase defect, an endometrial biopsy (which I had put off for months because I heard horror stories about the pain involved). I scheduled it for the fifth of August. This procedure entails a pelvic exam where the doctor extracts a small sample of uterine lining via a soft, straw-like catheter with no anesthesia while you are lying spread-eagle on a cold examination table. The tissue is then examined under a microscope to see if the hormone levels that affect the endometrium (lining) are in balance. The procedure causes some cramping in most cases. *Sounds fun, huh?* I decided it was time to be brave and exhaust all possible causes of my recurrent miscarriages.

Friday, July 25, 2003

I have an endometrial biopsy scheduled for August 5 to check for luteal phase defect (one of the final tests I'll be having except for additional immunology testing), and I hope to God they find a luteal phase defect so at least it can be fixed. However, I have had progesterone support with two of my chemical pregnancies, and it didn't work. I've heard, though, that sometimes, they give you another drug in conjunction with the progesterone (like Lupron or hCG) to treat luteal phase defect. If that test shows up normal, then I'll have to move on to detailed immunological testing (I've already had some of them) and travel across the country for it (Chicago), which my DH also balks at. If you've read this far, bless your patience!!

I just needed to vent out my frustrations. I've already had a nice crying session this morning. You'd think after an AHC followed by five miscarriages, I'd give up, but I guess I'm just a glutton for punishment. Any advice or thoughts would be greatly appreciated.

Wednesday, August 6, 2003

I had my endometrial biopsy yesterday, and it wasn't as bad as I thought it would be. It was pretty uncomfortable, but nothing excruciating. Luckily, I didn't have any cramping afterward and minimal brief spotting. Now I have to wait two wks. (from yesterday) to get the results in a phone consult with my RE. I'm hoping beyond hope that they make a diagnosis of luteal phase defect since that is something that is pretty easily corrected. I would be so happy if they could actually find an answer to all my M/Cs. I'm relieved it's over. I had heard nightmare stories about it. I hate being in this holding phase while awaiting test results. I wish I could immediately start TTC again, but don't want to till I have all avenues covered. Hope everyone is doing okay.

To add to my disappointment, the endometrial biopsy also showed that my uterine lining was "in phase" (normal). So, no luteal phase defect for me. I bristled with irritation when my color Doppler ultrasound studies yielded normal results as well. I was frustrated beyond belief. I know it sounds crazy to be disappointed when the doctor reports that your test results are normal, but as anyone who has experienced infertility will tell you, finding a problem is bliss because it can possibly be *fixed.* Dr. Brown gave me a mere 10 percent chance of having a baby with my own eggs and advised me that donor egg would be my best chance for success.

Until someone goes through something unimaginable, they cannot speak to what they would do in that situation. One must experience it oneself to grasp the reality of the nightmare.

Saturday, August 2, 2003

I'm sorry about your sister's insensitive comments. People who haven't been through what we have just don't "get it." I was at a gathering with some friends the other night, and one of my friends commented that she would never have an abortion. She was talking to someone else, and this comment really stung me. I almost said something, but just let it go. Other people truly don't understand the effect their words can have on us....

Wednesday, November 12, 2003
I had a similar situation arise with my best friend a few months ago. I terminated due to trisomy 13 back in Jan. 2000, and she fully supported my decision and said she would do the same if her baby had a trisomy (including Down syndrome). Well, she got pregnant by "accident" a few months ago with her third child (which was hard for me to take as it is) and we were talking on the phone one night, and she said that her husband was insisting that she get an amnio and she didn't know if she wanted to do that—that she wasn't sure she could go through with terminating if there was a problem. She also went on to say that her mother told her that if she ever terminated a pregnancy for any reason, that she'd never speak to her again, and went on to mention that her friend (who I think is very judgmental) said, "Why would you get an amnio? You know you wouldn't do anything about it if anything were wrong, anyway." I told her that her comments were upsetting to me and that I didn't need to hear things like that, and that I wouldn't feel comfortable being around her mother in the future (her mother is at many of the social gatherings that my friend has). I thought it was extremely insensitive of her to share these things with me, which were very hurtful to me. She knew I was upset because I abruptly said, "I have to go now," on the phone. She did end up sending me an e-card apology the next day. We are still friends, but I have since distanced myself from her (her accidental pregnancy is too hard for me to take right now, and the comments are kind of etched in my memory). I do truly understand where you're coming from and the hurt you're feeling. I used to be pretty open about our decision to terminate but now find myself not telling people and

just talking about my "miscarriages." I think the bottom line is that no one can completely understand unless they've been in our shoes, and they tend to say the wrong things sometimes (not necessarily intentionally). Please try to hang in there and know that I can totally relate to you.

❧

Grasping at straws, I expanded my research to a new level. I scoured the internet for hours and hours trying to solve the puzzle to the reason for my repeat miscarriages. I found an article claiming that ingesting NutraSweet could attack the early embryo. Unconvinced that low sperm morphology could not be the culprit in chromosomally defective conceptions, I searched in vain for information to refute this. I looked at getting further, more detailed immunological testing that would involve travel to Chicago or California to meet with the "experts." I was a desperate woman.

Tuesday, September 2, 2003

I'm really sorry that it appears you've had a chemical PG this month. I can relate, having had five of them! It truly sucks! Does your doctor think that chem. PGs are egg issues? Mine does. Why did your doctor refer you to a regular endocrinologist (versus RE)? What other types of tests are they going to do? I'm just curious cause I'm grasping to find answers. My AF is due on Thursday, and although we don't use birth control anymore, I've lost hope. I don't even think I ovulated this month 'cause I didn't get the usual signs. I'm seriously considering donor egg myself (after I get some final immunological tests done). I'm just awaiting the medical records I requested from my RE's office, and then I'm making a phone appt. with Dr. Carter in Chicago to get the comprehensive testing. This certainly is a long, tiring journey, that's for sure! Hope you're keeping your spirits up somewhat. I'm trying.

❦

An invitation arrived in the mail for my cousin Connor's wedding to take place on September 6, 2003, in Martha's Vineyard, Massachusetts. His father and my uncle, Ben, one of my favorite uncles growing up, raised his family of five kids in Martha's Vineyard, and I had many fond memories of my several visits to the island over the years. The quaintness and beauty of this small strip of land was just the getaway I craved to help ease my burdens.

My cousin Lexie and I, both with a strong sense of family ties and always ready for an adventure, decided to set out on the twelve-hour journey up the East Coast with her at the wheel, the last leg of the expedition culminating in a forty-five-minute ferry ride from Boston, Massachusetts, to Woods Hole, Martha's Vineyard. I have gone the prop plane route before from Boston to the island but did not wish to endure the noisy, claustrophobic, turbulent "death-wish trip" again. Flying makes me edgy anyway, especially in a tin can with a propeller reverberating in my throat.

The first evening, we ate a docile dinner out at a restaurant in town where Uncle Ben, and two of his sons, Jason and John, and daughter, Monica, joined us. In the restaurant, Uncle Ben lifted his shirt and displayed his nipple ring and other piercings to us with pride, signaling a new phase in his life. It was enjoyable catching up with everyone and seeing the miraculous transformation of my first cousins from children to young adults; years had passed since I last saw them.

Ben ran into a friend in the restaurant, a local flower-child type. She invited us over to her Haight-Ashbury-style abode, decked out in hippie beads and incense. We sat around and swigged Heinekens and listened to my cousin Monica's folk music CD that she recorded in California. I ineptly smoked cigarettes (a true red flag that I'd had one too many) and blew smoke rings, dropping an ember onto the carpet in the process. This sent me into a fit of laughter and a heroic cleanup attempt with a dousing of beer. This behavior is so out of character for me; I was not in my right mind. The flower child was not impressed.

The second night, Friday, Lexie and I attended an informal, cookout-style rehearsal dinner at the home of the bride-to-be, Melanie. As the wine flowed, my shyness transformed into sociability. Ben's wife, Janice, and I connected over glass after glass of wine as we bonded over marriage and miscarriages.

As the party concluded, we were all loitering in the street outside the house and chatting it up. Connor and his grooms-men were discussing which local watering hole they were getting ready to hit. I, in my "party mode," asked if Lexie and I could join them, to which we got half-hearted affirmations. Lexie had the wherewithal to suggest that we should do our own thing, to which I am sure they were grateful beyond measure. I am positive the last thing Connor wanted was to have two middle-aged cousins in tow, tagging along on his last guys' night out as a single man.

I tend to "hoot and holler" when I have had too much to drink, and my voice rose a few too many decibels over the limit of "disturbing the peace" at that hour. One of the bridesmaids stuck her head out of the upstairs window and told us in no uncertain terms that if we did not keep it down, Melanie would call the police. I am sure that my voice was the determining factor.

Lexie and I ended up barhopping with cousin Monica in downtown Martha's Vineyard for a couple of hours. I do not remember too much of the evening after that, except puking in an alley while Monica held my hair away from my face while I lamented my all-too-familiar abortion and miscarriage(s) saga to her through a stream of tears. *Nothing like catching up after all these years in this fashion, huh?* So much for making a good impression—maybe a lasting one, but not a good one. Monica, a free spirit, was living in Southern California at the time and trying to break into the singing business, so I am sure not too much judgment was passed, but still.

The wedding was held the next afternoon in a gorgeous outdoor setting, and I made sure to behave in a noble manner, only allowing myself one beer for the whole event. I am sure the bride, Melanie, was shaking in her boots the whole time, thinking the wayward housewife cousin from the DC area was going to break rowdy at her nuptials.

On Sunday, Lexie and I bade our farewells (much to the relief of the bride and residents of Martha's Vineyard, I'm sure) and missed the ferry while we were shopping in the ferry gift shop as our car sat parked in the lineup. After pulling a few strings (Lexie crying to the ferry supervisor), we were able to hitch a ride on the next one, the truck ferry.

The trip was a rather humiliating experience for me, to say the least, and will not be marked as one of the prouder events of my life. I pictured my "Most Wanted" mug shot being plastered all over Martha's Vineyard post office walls and grocery stores in the aftermath of my departure. By the time September 2003 rolled around, I had experienced enough misfortune to drive Annette Funicello of the *Mickey Mouse Club* Mouseketeers to popping Prozac.

None of these practices were beneficial to my mental state, but they were all part of the process.

⁓

Mark even said he would use donor sperm, if necessary.

> *Monday, September 22, 2003*
>
> *Last night, my DH and I had an in-depth discussion, and he has agreed to let me try this last attempt with donor egg and donor sperm. My RE believes that all of my chemical PGs are due to chromosomally damaged eggs, so she is all for donor egg. My DH also has extremely low sperm morphology (only 3 percent), which I believe could be contributing to my chemical PGs. I think they're just fertilizing weakly, either due to my aged eggs or his defective sperm (What a pair we are, right?!)*

Soon after, we found out that our insurance did not cover any of the donor costs (which would have been almost $13,000 for a sole donor cycle), so we held off on the plan of donor egg for the time being.

It is amazing that Mark stayed with me after all I put him through. I know I was not an easy person to live with. I figured if our marriage could sustain itself after all this, it was as solid as an oak tree.

CHAPTER 8

More IVF

*Work begins when the fear of doing nothing at
all finally trumps the terror of doing it badly.*
~Alain de Botton

My RE believed a donor egg IVF cycle would be our best option at this point. She informed us the clinical pregnancy rates are 60–70 percent per attempt with this type of IVF. However, my gung-ho plans for doing donor egg IVF were shot down when I discovered my health insurance did not cover donor costs, which were close to $13,000 for one cycle in 2003. The outlay of funds could not be justified for the odds of success. So I figured since I had two remaining "regular" IVF attempts covered by insurance in their entirety, I might as well take advantage of them. Based on my past fruitless attempts at childbearing, I expected it to be a waste of time but not money.

I figured the odds of this second IVF working were as probable as

1. finding the Holy Grail;

2. solving Rubik's Cube in ten minutes or less;

3. grasping a stuffed animal prize with the mechanical claw on the first try;

4. hitting a home run at Wrigley Field; and

5. getting a marriage proposal from Matthew McConaughey.

Tuesday, September 30, 2003

Congrats on finding a donor! It sounds like things will be moving along very quickly. That's great news! I wish you the best of luck! We are still thinking about donor egg, but since our insurance doesn't cover any of the donor costs (and I found out they'd be almost $13,000 for a sole donor cycle!), we've decided to do a regular IVF next month with my eggs (since I have two regular IVFs left, paid 100 percent by my insurance). My AF is due in two days, and I should be starting BCPs [birth control pills] the following Tuesday. They anticipate a retrieval of around Nov. 18, so it looks like we will be cycle buddies!

Again, a big congrats to you!

ℰℑ

I awaited the arrival of my next period with the adrenaline-fueled anticipation of Olympic swimmer Michael Phelps at the 2004 Athens Olympics, positioned at the starting block, ears trained to the screeching blare of the signal, dreaming of his first gold.

My period heralded its arrival on October 4. The first drug introduced in the IVF process was the birth control pill. My doctor prescribed Desogen. I swallowed my first pill on October 9, five days after my period started, per procedure. My regimen consisted of three weeks of birth control pills, an irony considering I was trying to embark upon pregnancy, not prevent it, but who was I to question medical authority? Dr. Brown later explained that the purpose of the pill was to control the timing of the IVF cycle. For the next two weeks, I took one pill every morning.

October 23 marked the first day of many injections to come, which for me was the most tedious and feared part of the IVF process. My initial dosage of Lupron was ten units (.1 mL). This drug helps to suppress some of the naturally occurring hormones that control the reproductive cycle so that ovulation will not occur. I soon learned to make friends with Lupron, incorporating it into my morning ritual like a cup of coffee—it was how I started my day for many days to come (twenty-five days, it turned out). It is simple and involves little pain since it is injected just under the skin (not into muscle). With practice, it became as routine as brushing my teeth. For seven days, I took Lupron in conjunction with the birth control pill.

I include all the tedious steps of the IVF process to assist other women going through this. It is a daunting undertaking that requires intensive study of the step-by-step procedures outlined in the thick manual. If someone had spelled it out for me like this before I delved into the intimidating journey, it would have been invaluable.

That first morning, I flicked off the metal top on the bottle of premixed Lupron, revealing a black rubber cap. I wiped the rubber top with an alcohol pad to maintain sterility. Each kit came with fourteen needles, and I ripped open the package, selected a needle, and removed the orange cap. Next, I pulled off the cap on the bottom of the syringe. I inserted the needle into the center of the rubber cap and turned the bottle of liquid upside down. I drew back the plunger to a little more than ten units (.1 cc), then pushed it back up to the ten-unit mark. Then, I flicked the bottle with the tip of my index finger to remove any bubbles. I ripped open another alcohol pad and rubbed it around in a circular motion at a large area around the injection site (the meaty part of my thigh between the top of my leg and knee was my site of choice). I fanned the leg with my hand to allow the alcohol to dry so the shot would not sting. I picked up the syringe with my right hand and positioned the eye of the needle (the beveled end) up toward the ceiling. I pinched up the thigh skin at the injection site with my left hand and plunged the needle directly into my skin like a dart. *Whew! I did it.* Sounds like a lengthy process, but once I got the hang of it, it proved to be easy.

I took my last birth control pill on October 29, and from October 30 through November 4, I injected Lupron in the mornings.

After fourteen days on Lupron (which corresponds to around day five of the menstrual period), I started my morning monitoring at GIVF to check my uterine lining and ovaries and began my FSH injections. These are the fertility drugs that (hopefully) harvest numerous ripe eggs for the pickin'. GIVF, which I visited several mornings a week to monitor the progress of my eggs, became my second home; I was there at the ungodly hour of 7:00 a.m. so I could get to work by 8:00 a.m. My response to the drugs in my prior IVF was stellar, given the fact that I was ancient by childbearing standards.

I deployed the big guns on November 5, at Lupron day fourteen. At 6:40 p.m., I began preparations. I scrubbed the kitchen counter with Formula 409, dried it, and marched over to the fridge. I selected three vials of Gonal-F and one vial of sodium chloride and carried them to the table as if they were live grenades. I reached under my kitchen cabinet for the white cake box and pulled out the clear 3 cc syringe, the 3 cc turquoise syringe with attached 23-gauge one-and-a-half-inch needle, an insulin syringe with a 26-gauge needle, 1-inch 19-gauge filter needle, a couple of alcohol swabs, and a Band-Aid for good measure. Let me tell you, the first time I laid my eyes on that filter needle, I was thinking, *I'm not launching that damn scud missile into* my *leg.* This was before I knew it was not meant for injecting into me.

I washed and dried my hands with soap and water with care. I picked up the glass Gonal-F vial, flicked the powder so it was all below the blue dot on the vial, pressed my thumb against the dot, and pushed straight back, snapping the glass neck of the ampule. I repeated this process for the remaining two ampules (amps) of Gonal-F and the liquid vial of sodium chloride, careful to tap any liquid below the blue dot before snapping off the top of the sodium chloride. My dosage was three amps (225 IU) of Gonal-F mixed with one amp (1 cc) of sodium chloride. I opened the 3 cc syringe with 23-gauge needle (mixing needle) from its package and withdrew 1 cc from the sodium chloride vial. I injected the liquid down the side of the first Gonal-F powder ampule and rolled the vial between my fingers with a gentle motion to mix it. I took the mixing needle, drew up the contents of the first vial, and injected it into the second Gonal-F vial. I mixed the second vial, withdrew its contents with the mixing needle, injected its contents into the third vial of Gonal-F, and mixed it. I unwrapped the 3 cc syringe and filter needle, removed the cap, and attached the filter needle to the syringe in a twisting motion. I inserted the filter needle into the final mixed Gonal-F solution and drew up the medication (to filter out any glass particles). Next, I unwrapped the subcutaneous (sub-Q) needle, removed the filter needle, and attached the sub-Q needle to the filled syringe. I held the syringe with the needle pointing upward, tapped the barrel of the syringe to get the air bubbles to the end of it, and gently depressed the syringe to remove the bubbles.

I took a deep breath to relax, pinched up the skin on my thigh, and plunged the magical potion into my thigh. I depressed the plunger with steady pressure, felt the sting of multiple bees, and chanted, "Baby, baby, baby…" to ease the pain of the cause.

After the Gonal-F, I administered my Repronex injection (75 IU, or one vial) mixed with 1 cc of sodium chloride. The preparation procedures were similar to that of Gonal-F, except no filter needle was needed, and I rolled the Repronex/sodium chloride solution sideways to mix.

By the way, one of the fringe benefits of taking fertility drugs is the night sweats that make you wake up with your nightgown stuck to your skin like a wet paper towel. You feel like you are in the midst of a menopausal nightmare.

❧

On the second day of taking FSH, I reduced my dosage of Lupron by half to .05 mL. I gave myself one Gonal-F injection and one Repronex injection every evening between 6:00 p.m. and 8:00 p.m. for eleven days.

On day ten of fertility shots, I realized with horror that I was out of Gonal-F. I had one refill left on my prescription, but since it was mail order, I knew it would never arrive by the next day. I phoned the GIVF nurse in a panic, and she told me I could get more of the medication at the pharmacy they used—Merrifield CVS. The next day, I made the forty-five-minute trek to Falls Church, Virginia, for my emergency supply of Gonal-F.

On November 15, I trudged into GIVF for my blood work and ultrasound to check the estrogen (E2) levels and follicle growth. The technician noted fourteen follicles measuring between 13.5 mm and 18 mm, which was ideal, and measured my uterine lining at 11.6 mm, an optimal thickness. They scheduled my hCG trigger shot (to give ovulation a swift shove over the side of the cliff) for midnight the following night. This is the phase of IVF that we all wait for, like the grand finale in a Fourth of July fireworks display or the opening ceremony of the Olympics. *Let the games begin*, I thought.

Sunday, November 16, 2003

I've been lurking for a while now and just wanted to give an update on my IVF. I'm scheduled to do my hCG trigger shot tonight at midnight, and my retrieval is Tuesday morning at 11 a.m. On the last sonogram, there were fourteen follicles, and they said my uterine lining is nice and thick (11.6). I'll be doing a two-day transfer (on Thursday) and then the 2WW. I'm so happy to have all these shots almost over with. My bruised legs are happy, too! After my AHC (in Jan. 2001) and five chemical PGs in a row (one being from an IVF/PGD cycle), I'm holding out a shred of hope that this one will work. Wish me luck.

On the morning of November 16, I administered my twenty-fifth and final Lupron injection of this IVF cycle. I fretted all day over the impending hCG trigger shot—not over the actual injection, but the preparation. From my prior experience with the IUI and PGD/IVF, I recalled the tedious steps involved in capturing this precious liquid medication at the precise time. Talk about pressure.

First, I withdrew 1 cc of sterile water from the bottle with a 22-gauge syringe with a 1–1½ inch needle, pierced the needle through the rubber stopper at the top of the bottle containing the hCG powder, and injected the liquid down the side. Using caution, I rolled the bottle sideways between my hands for about thirty seconds until the powder dissolved, hyperaware that if the bottle were to slip out of my hands and crash to the floor, my dreams would shatter along with the glass. Then, I turned the bottle with the attached needle upside down and withdrew the liquid. *Sounds simple enough, right?* Not. Attempting to draw up as much of the solution as possible without growing large air bubbles in the syringe (not a good thing) with the clock ticking closer and closer to the midnight injection deadline was likened to trying to squeeze Winnie-the-Pooh back out through the front door of Rabbit's house, as any fellow IVFer will attest. After several trembling attempts accompanied by a sweat-beaded brow, *voila!* After I flicked the sides to get rid of small air bubbles (tiny, champagne-like bubbles are okay), the syringe was ready for action. I changed to a 26-gauge syringe with ⅝-inch needle, rubbed my thigh with an alcohol pad, pinched up the fat of my thigh (not a problem for me to find), and plunged in the "ovarian epinephrine."

The next day and a half were like static on a television set late at night after broadcasting has been cut off, a state of purgatory awaiting the next phase.

On Monday, November 17, I took an HPT first thing in the morning to make sure it was positive (to prove the hCG was in my system from the trigger shot) and called GIVF to alert them of the reading. Next on my agenda were three Betadine douches (morning, afternoon, and evening) to ensure my female areas were sanitized prior to my retrieval the following morning. This fun-filled task involved clamping the hose on the douche bag *(pardon the expression)*, filling the bag with the one-ounce Betadine packet and up to three-fourths full of tap water, hanging the bag high up on top of the shower door, inserting the tube vaginally, sitting back and relaxing *(yeah, right!)*, releasing the switch to the floodgates, and *whoosh!* I realized later that day that Betadine ruins clothes, as the stain would not come out of my underwear.

My final task for the night was to avoid food and water after midnight (easy enough compared to the other steps). Mark's instruction for the evening was to service himself ("Okay, if I *must*") and then refrain from such activity until his andrology appointment the next morning at 10:30 a.m. My retrieval was set for 11:00 a.m.

We arrived at GIVF at 10:00 a.m. the next morning (November 18) as we were instructed to show up one hour before the scheduled retrieval time. I was filled with nervous excitement. Mark headed over to the andrology lab (in walking distance) at 10:15 a.m. to perform his manly duties in the comfort of the private lounge stocked with plenty of visual stimulation.

I was led into an exam room on the second floor, signed

consent forms, and listened as Dr. Lennox, who would perform the procedure, explained the steps. The nurse started an IV in my arm and told me she was administering midazolam and morphine to relax me. "My chest feels some pressure," I said.

"That's normal when the morphine first goes in," she said, which allayed my concerns. All I remember is a vague, faraway pain as my ovaries were plucked and saying "ouch" in my dreams. I remained in the recovery room for about one hour, and then Mark drove us home, me feeling worn out from the harvest.

Later that afternoon, I called GIVF for a progress report. The nurse told me that they retrieved twenty eggs, an abundant number.

Tuesday, November 18, 2003

I went for my egg retrieval at 11:00 a.m. this morning, and they retrieved twenty eggs, fifteen of which were mature. She said that was a good response for my age of thirty-nine. I'm keeping my fingers crossed that one will decide to "stick around." My transfer will be Friday (they started doing three-day transfers at Genetics & IVF Institute).

༒

The night after retrieval, I began a round of tetracycline (to avoid infection) for five days. I also started taking progesterone (Prometrium vaginal tablets) three times a day to be taken until a negative beta hCG blood pregnancy test or until ten weeks pregnant, if I was lucky enough. I also self-medicated with an 81 milligram St. Joseph baby aspirin (the yummy orange taste conjures up fond childhood memories) once a day as an added insurance policy, as I had heard that its blood-thinning properties might prevent miscarriage.

My transfer was first scheduled for Friday, November 21, but was rescheduled to Thursday, November 20.

Wednesday, November 19, 2003

I got the call this afternoon that out of fifteen mature eggs, fourteen were fertilized. We did IVF with ICSI since my DH has low sperm morphology. My last IVF had a fertilization rate of 66 percent, and this time it was 93 percent. Not sure why it was higher this time. The only thing my DH has been doing differently is eating a low fat, low sodium, and low cholesterol diet due to slightly elevated cholesterol levels. Maybe this had an impact. My transfer has been scheduled for tomorrow at 12:45 p.m. (they decided to do a two-day versus three-day transfer). They will give me an update in the morning on the grading of the embryos and which ones stopped developing. Hopefully, I will have some to freeze for another cycle if this one doesn't work.

CHAPTER 9

Nirvana

Take into account that great love and
great achievements involve great risk.

~Dalai Lama

On November 20, 2003, I lay on the cold exam table at GIVF with Mark at my side. Today was the big day. Eleven embryos of good quality were suitable for transfer. My bladder cried out for release from the thirty-two ounces of water ingested over the past hour, per doctor instructions.

"I suggest transferring three or four embryos. What do you think?" asked Dr. Bowers.

I am of the mindset that in the world of gambling, you should stack your odds. "Put five back in," I said.

The doctor digested this request for a few seconds, then said, "Given your age and history, I don't think that's unreasonable."

My husband's face turned as white as a baby's butt doused in baby powder. "*Five?*" he asked, his face holding the gaze of a cornered, helpless rodent.

"Yes, five," I said, determination cementing my face. Mark knows when I set my mind to something, there's no arguing. Mark met my proclamation with the enthusiasm evoked from the splash caused by the hasty backlash of a toilet plunger retracted from the bowl.

"Okay. Let's do it then," said Dr. Bowers. "Please remain very still. I will be transferring four 4-cell embryos and one 6-cell embryo." To my amazement, the wall behind the doctor transformed into a sliding door that opened to a clandestine lab, something straight out of the Starship Enterprise from *Star Trek*. Captain Kirk handed Dr. Spock the mysterious vial through the opening, whose contents contained my destiny. At that moment in time, I was enraptured by the sci-fi operation and the fact that cells were dividing in that container. Five little lives were about to merge with mine.

I lay as still as a corpse, not wanting to jostle anything as the catheter was guided into my uterus with care. Dr. Bowers inserted the tiny embryos into me, and I felt a smattering of hope, a glimmer of life, a leap of faith.

As instructed, I lay on the table for fifteen minutes. "How long do I have to wait before I can use the bathroom?" I asked.

"You can go as soon as you leave the exam table," said Dr. Bowers, "and here is a souvenir for you." He handed me an ultrasound picture showing five arrows pointing to each embryo and the words "Good luck" scrolled across (see next page). *If this works*, I thought, *how many people can say they have a picture of their own implantation?*

I tiptoed to the bathroom with the grace of a prima ballerina; I tread with the caution of a doctor carrying a kidney off the helicopter launch pad. I peed without using any muscles or force, letting it trickle without coaxing. I could not help but think the embryos were flowing right out of me and into the commode. *Stop these nonproductive thoughts*, I told myself.

I requested that the remaining six embryos be frozen; in all likelihood, I would be using them for the third IVF attempt. GIVF charged $40 per month for their rent.

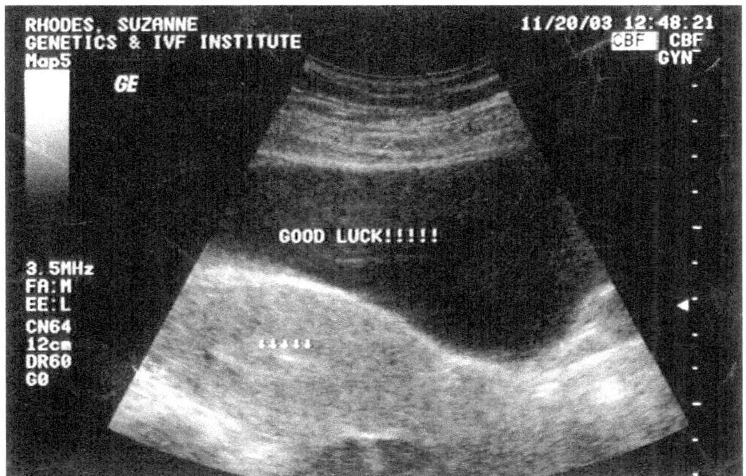

It was November 29, three days before my scheduled beta hCG blood test (that indicates the level of three pregnancy hormones: hCG, progesterone, and estrogen). Against my better judgment, I took the fifty-sixth First Response HPT in my reproductive career *(slight exaggeration)*. I kept First Response in business. I blew through their pregnancy tests like others blow through sticks of chewing gum. I could finance my firstborn child's college education with the money I spent on these tests. I chided myself for this home pregnancy test addiction. I tried to kick the habit, but it was useless; I was a hopeless addict. I had a track record of staring at numerous First Response Pregnancy Test results with the early morning light shining through the window, straining my eyes to see a second pink line like a mirage in the desert.

Two days later, on December 1, I caved and got another fix. I made a pit stop at the CVS drugstore in Chantilly and snatched up another First Response Pregnancy Test. I rushed home, peed on the stick, and the second line blazed with a brilliant pink hue after a mere twenty seconds. I repressed excitement when the second pink line appeared in the window; I had been burned too many times.

Monday, December 1, 2003

I took an HPT two days ago, and it showed a positive. I took another this morning, and it showed a very dark line after only twenty seconds. I go in tomorrow morning for my official beta hCG blood test by my infertility clinic. After five chemical PGs in a row, I'm not getting excited yet. However, with all my chemical PGs, the line was already fading by now, so it appears that the hCG levels are still rising. I'm keeping my fingers crossed that I get some good solid hCG numbers tomorrow. I had five embryos transferred, so it's a little scary. Will let you know tomorrow afternoon what my numbers show. (Not excited, but have a faint sliver of hope.)

❧

The morning of December 2, I made the forty-five-minute trek to GIVF for the official pregnancy blood test. I waited all day with anticipation yet realism. *Don't get your hopes up,* I thought.

After I'd quit my job in telecommunications, I babysat and pet-sat/dog-walked to make some income. I worked for a woman who operated a business out of Bristow, Virginia, and several of her jobs were in my neighborhood, South Riding. A dog-sitting client was to arrive at my house at 2:00 p.m. for a consultation on a job to watch his two black labs, Buster and Finn. I thought it was a coincidence when I learned this client was my neighbor who lived right behind me.

The doorbell rang at 2:00 p.m. sharp, and I greeted Chuck Simmons. I led him to the kitchen table, where I spread out the contract. "I'm taking the family on a Western Caribbean cruise over Christmas," he said.

"That's great," I said, "I'm jealous." As I explained the rates and jotted down his dogs' names and feeding schedules, the phone begged to be answered. Under normal circumstances, I would never interrupt a business meeting to answer the phone, *but this wasn't normal circumstances.*

"Excuse me, do you mind if I take this call? I'm waiting for a call from my doctor's office," I said, hoping he would not be put off.

"No problem," he said, being a congenial guy.

"Hello?"

"Is this Mrs. Rhodes?" asked the GIVF nurse.

"Yes, it is."

"I have the results of your beta hCG test, and the level is 167."

"You're kidding?"

"Yes, they're 167. That's a good number," she said.

"Thank you so much," I said.

Well, I may as well have just received the news that I won the lottery. I wanted to jump up on the kitchen table, hoot and holler, and dance a jig, but I thought better of it, as the neighbor might have called the little men in starched overcoats to take me away in a straitjacket.

I turned to Chuck after I hung up, and to contain my euphoria would not have done the moment justice. Bouncing with electricity and knowing full well it was not professional (and I could not have cared less), I shared my news with him. "I just had IVF, and I'm pregnant and my pregnancy blood test results showed high numbers, which is good. I'm so excited 'cause I've had five miscarriages in a row and have never gotten this far." What a mouthful. I am sure this was not what he bargained for when he came over for the meeting.

Being the good-natured man and neighbor that he was, he smiled. "Congratulations. That's great news." A successful, productive meeting indeed.

Tuesday, December 2, 2003

I'm in shock right now. My doctor's office called, and my beta hCG level is 167! With my five previous chemical PGs, my betas only got up to fifteen or sixteen at this point. She said my estrogen and progesterone levels are also good. She wants me to come back in two days for another blood test and said my numbers looked so good. She said it's probably one, but could be two with this hCG number. I know it's too early for me to get excited, but I've passed one hurdle already by having viable hCG numbers. I never thought I'd even make it this far.

❧

On December 4, I drove to GIVF's alternate office in Ashburn, Virginia, for my repeat beta hCG test (to ensure that my pregnancy hormone levels were doubling every two days). Dr. Brown threw her arms around me in congratulations when I walked in the door. She marveled at my strong initial beta hCG numbers on the chart she held.

❧

"Mark, I'm nervous. I hope they see a heartbeat," I said as I perched on the end of the exam table awaiting the ultrasound technician at Washington Radiology.

"I'm sure they will," said Mark. "You've had a lot of morning sickness, and that's a good sign, isn't it?"

"That's true," I said.

The sonographer walked through the door and introduced herself as Tanya. "I'm going to check for a fetal pole and heartbeat and make sure everything appears to be on track," she said. Several thoughts dashed across my consciousness: Please let there be a heartbeat; let the baby's measurements be correct; don't let there be more than two beating hearts, or Mark will freak.

Seeing the kaleidoscope of my baby's flickering heart was like marveling at Monet's *Water Lilies* for the first time; hearing that my baby's measurements were normal was a symphony to my ears.

Friday, December 19, 2003

I had my six-week sonogram yesterday, and we saw a heartbeat! All measurements were normal, and it was just one (much to my husband's relief—they put five embryos in for the IVF)! I am having morning sickness and am very grateful for it. It has been three years since my AHC due to trisomy 13, and I had been trying for another two-and-a-half years. After five chemical PGs that I lost only one week after the PG test turned positive, I've now made it farther than I ever have (since AHC). I hope this can offer a glimmer of hope to those of you that think it may never happen again. For two-and-a-half years, I've seen almost everyone pass me up to have a pregnancy post-AHC, and thought it unfair that it wasn't happening for me. I guess persistence paid off. I just kept plugging away over and over again and wouldn't give up. I know I'm nowhere near out of the woods yet, but am just so thankful to have made it this far….

A numerical flip chart that tallied viable pregnancies had mocked me on the Genetics & IVF Institute (GIVF) waiting room wall at every morning monitoring appointment. Its four bold, black numbers stared me down, and they won. They were a constant reminder of everyone else's fortune and my failure. I dreamed of being the one to initiate the simple yet loaded act of the receptionist getting up from her chair, walking over to the wall, and flipping the elusive number on the far right. She would not realize the significance of her simple actions at the time; to her, a number—to me, a dream fulfilled. In late December 2003, my number had finally flipped along with my heart, shocked back into rhythm, heralding my future child.

During my two-and-a-half years of trying for a baby, my emotions were up and down like a roller coaster, alternating between hope and despair. As I crossed my fingers, my eight-week ultrasound also yielded normal results. *Normal*, a mediocre word for most people, a *spectacular* word for me. When I got home, I gazed at the sonogram images. My eyes danced as they viewed the fuzzy images of life.

Thursday, January 1, 2004

I tried another IVF (without PGD) as a last-ditch effort in November (they put in five embryos). I became pregnant and am now about eight-and-a-half weeks pregnant (the farthest I've made it since my AHC). I've had two U/Ss, and at six wks. they saw the h/b and at my eight-wk. U/S, everything was still looking good. I'm keeping my fingers crossed that this is the one....

❧

My next two hurdles were the first OB appointment at ten weeks and a nuchal translucency (NT) test between ten and eleven weeks. The nuchal translucency test is an ultrasound performed in the first trimester to screen for trisomy 21 (Down syndrome), trisomy 18 (Edwards syndrome), trisomy 13 (Patau syndrome), and heart problems. It measures the baby's nasal bone as well as fluid behind the neck. A high volume of fluid can indicate problems.

Sunday, January 11, 2004

Thanks to all for their congratulations on my pregnancy. I'll be ten weeks on Tuesday and have my first OB appt. that day. I plan on having a nuchal translucency test between ten and eleven weeks (where they measure the fluid behind the baby's neck to check for increased risk of chromosome problems—if it's elevated). I'll most likely have an amnio at around sixteen wks. Am still having morning sickness, which is a good sign. I'm remaining hopeful that the baby is healthy.

At the first ten-week OB appointment, Dr. Grimes heard the heartbeat through the stethoscope, and my uterus measured within the proper range. However, doubts lurked and sliced through my contentment like a steak knife through cotton candy.

Friday, January 16, 2004

Congrats on the good U/S results. I had a really good attitude about the PG until this past week. Things are still going well, but my fears of chromosome problems are starting to surface now that it's getting closer to the time that I could do genetic testing. I'm hemming and hawing about whether or not I should have an amnio. I know I should (I'm thirty-nine) but am scared to death of miscarriage after having five in a row. I'm having the nuchal translucency test (where they measure fluid behind the baby's neck to check for possible chromosome problems) next Friday, and I will request a quad-screen test at fifteen wks. (I think that's when it's done). If they come back okay, I'll probably forgo the amnio. I'm scared to death they'll find elevated fluid levels next week (that's what indicated a problem last time). I understand your concerns. Now that I've seen/heard the h/b and seem to be getting past the M/C range, I'm starting to worry about everything else that can go wrong, so I completely understand your fears. I am due 8/11 and am ten-and-a-half wks., so we are pretty close together. I guess I'm just going to try my best to keep from obsessing about it and keep myself busy, but that's easier said than done. Good luck to you with the rest of your "hurdles."

❧

My heart surged with pleasure and relief when the specialist calibrated the nuchal translucency to be 0.5 mm. This was well below the normal range of 3.0 mm and under (anything over 3.0 mm can indicate a chromosome problem in some cases). My level was a 3.4 in my trisomy 13 pregnancy.

The baby was moving all over the place, and all the other measurements looked good. The specialist gave me a 90 percent chance of having a baby with no chromosome problems. A layer of my concerns peeled away like an onion skin.

❧

On February 10, 2004, I had my fourteen-week sonogram. The technician noted no abnormalities, and she informed me that the baby growing inside me was a boy. This was a bittersweet moment for me: another boy.

I adopted the theme song "With Arms Wide Open" by Creed for this pregnancy, as the lyrics revealed that the singer had just learned he was expecting a son. As the words washed through the speakers, I transformed into a puddle of liquid nirvana.

❧

"I knew it was too good to be true," I said to Mark when I returned home from my sixteen-week OB appointment.

"What do you mean?"

"Dr. Grimes went over the notes from my last sonogram at fourteen weeks, and he said I have a complete placenta previa."

"What's that?" he asked.

"It's where the placenta is totally lying on top of your cervix. It's supposed to be up on the uterine wall."

"What can happen?"

"You can have bleeding episodes, so you have to take it easy," I said.

"Well, don't worry too much about it. Just don't lift anything heavy," he said.

"Yeah, the doctor put me on pelvic rest. That means I can't lift anything over ten pounds, and no sex," I said.

"Okay," said Mark, "I'm sure everything will be all right."

"Yeah, the doctor said that a lot of people have previas early on, but that only about one or two percent will still have it at the time of delivery. He said most of the time, the baby moves upward toward the back of the uterus as the pregnancy progresses. He said if I still had it at delivery time, they'd have to do a C-section to prevent a lot of bleeding."

I parked myself in my office chair, and within minutes, my home computer unleashed the horrendous scenarios that we all fall victim to when researching symptoms or illnesses.

"Mark," I said, "I could bleed to death and lose the baby."

"Suzanne. You're always thinking the worst-case scenario. Stop looking at the internet."

Wednesday, February 25, 2004

I just got back from my sixteen-week OB appt. and the notes from my fourteen-week u/s show that I have a complete placenta previa. The u/s doc had mentioned that I had a low-lying placenta, but not to worry 'cause they migrate upward most of the time as the pregnancy progresses. I am more concerned now that the notes show that he saw a complete placenta previa. I've read horror stories on the internet about hemorrhaging, etc., and I've also read that a complete (versus partial) previa usually doesn't correct itself. As if I didn't have enough to worry about! I also had my triple screen blood test today, so waiting for the results will be another thing to worry about. Since I'm thirty-nine, I'm sure I'll get a positive screening. Sorry to sound so negative. I'm just starting to worry.

❧

I had the triple screen test at sixteen weeks plus one day into my pregnancy. My doctor recommended the test no sooner than sixteen weeks to avoid false positives. Faithful to my bad luck streak, my triple screen test, which checks for spina bifida and Down syndrome, came back positive for Down syndrome; my baby had a one in seventy chance of the abnormality. This news was as welcome as a fruitcake on Christmas Eve. *But of course. Why not? Hadn't I experienced my share of bad things? Enough already.* I scheduled my amnio.

Wednesday, March 3, 2004

Well, in addition to having complete placenta previa, I just got my triple screen results back and had a positive screening for Down syndrome of one in seventy. They said my age-related odds at age thirty-nine were already one in ninety-two, and after the blood test, they are now one in seventy. Just my luck. I was babysitting two three yr. olds and a one yr. old when I got the wonderful news. Needless to say, I am very stressed out and just feel like

I can't win. I did have the good nuchal translucency test at eleven-and-a-half wks. that was only 0.5 mm, and the nasal bone was present (two Down syndrome markers that I don't have). However, I know that doesn't guarantee normal chromosomes. I am scheduled to have my amnio on Monday at 2:00 p.m. and hope to be able to get fluorescence in situ hybridization (FISH) results so I don't have to go crazy for two weeks. My OB said that the amnio should not complicate the placenta previa. I was already worried enough about the placenta previa, and now I have Down syndrome worries to add to the list. I wish I could just go to sleep for the next few days and wake up when they call with the results. I don't know how much more of this I can take. Does anyone know of someone who got one in seventy odds for Down syndrome and their baby didn't have it?

❧

On March 8, 2004, at eighteen weeks pregnant, I had my amnio at GIVF. Procedure-wise, no big deal; been there, done that. I was relieved to hear the placenta previa was marginal now (lying next to the cervix instead of on top of it). Afterward, the geneticist, Dr. Bowers, said, "Take it easy the rest of the day."

"I'm going on complete bed rest for two days just to be sure," I said.

"That's probably a good idea. This is a *premium pregnancy*," he said.

I requested FISH with the amnio, which gives preliminary results of the major chromosomal problems (trisomy

21, trisomy 13, and trisomy 18) and any issues with the sex chromosomes within forty-eight hours. My insurance did not cover FISH, which was $400 out of pocket, but at the time, that amount was as inconsequential as a lost penny down a sewer. I could not bear to face another two-week wait reminiscent of my two-week wait (that turned into three weeks) to receive my trisomy 13 sentence.

What followed were two days that dragged on, like being number 131 in the DMV queue when the attendant has just called number 2. Two days may as well have been two *decades*.

On March 10, 2004, I got the call that would exalt or extinguish my spirit in thirty seconds flat.

Wednesday, March 10, 2004

I got the call at three today that my FISH results were NORMAL!!!!!! I am beyond relieved, and this is the happiest I have felt in three years! I had the amnio on Monday, and I have more good news to report. My complete placenta previa has moved. It was completely covering the cervix and is now just sitting next to the cervix, but no part of the placenta is covering it anymore. They expect it to move even more over the coming weeks as my uterus grows. The baby is measuring six days ahead of schedule, so my due date is now August 5. We are having a boy!!! That is special since the baby we lost to trisomy 13 was a boy. I was so nervous all day waiting for the results, and now my relief is overwhelming. I have had no complications from the amnio—no cramping whatsoever. I just came off forty-eight hrs. of total bed rest (I took a very conservative approach). Thank you to everyone who wished me good luck with the amnio!

March 10, 2004, was one of the most rewarding days of my life. Seven days later, the final amnio report came in with a thumbs-up. *Triumph.*

I still needed some handholding throughout the remainder of my pregnancy. I shelled out cash every month in exchange for daily reassurance.

Doppler monitor to hear baby's heartbeat on command: $30 per month.

Reassurance: Priceless.

Thursday, March 18, 2004

I rented a fetal Doppler monitor (BabyBeat Doppler) a couple of weeks ago, and it costs $30 a month. To me, it's the best money I've ever spent. I rented it because of my low-lying placenta and not being able to feel as much movement because of it. It has been very reassuring to me, especially in light of all the problems I've had over the last three yrs. The first time I used it, it took a while to locate the baby's heartbeat due to lack of experience with the Doppler. However, once I found it, it has been easy to locate it every time. You just have to make sure it's the baby's heartbeat you're hearing and not your own. Your own is about half as slow as the baby's. The baby's sounds like a galloping horse. Also, since the baby moves around quite a bit, you may hear it for a few seconds and then lose it due to the baby changing locations. You can also hear the baby kicking in there. It is really cool. They send an instruction DVD to listen to that helps you distinguish the different sounds. You can also hear the placenta functioning, which sounds like wind blowing through trees. I finally started feeling pretty regular movement about a *week ago but still like to use it frequently (especially when I haven't felt the baby move in a few hours). To order, just go to babybeat.com. I ordered the simplest one, and it works great and is easy to use. I hope you get to hear your good amnio results really soon!*

❦

My final hurdle was the twenty-week anatomical level 3 ultrasound that checks all the baby's body structures/systems. This was the last peek through the window of the solar system that was my uterus. The placenta previa no longer existed, and all systems were a "go."

Tuesday, March 23, 2004

I had my twenty-week level 3 ultrasound today, and everything looked perfect! Also, my placenta previa has completely resolved itself. I am overwhelmed with relief and will actually start enjoying the rest of my pregnancy. I wish everyone else on this board good test results as well. We all deserve it after what we've been through.

❦

Months later, I waddled through my mom's front door into the foyer of her split-level house and took measured footsteps down the stairway to the basement where my anxious fans were waiting. Early in my pregnancy, I adopted the walk of a ninety-year-old woman, holding the banister like a lifeline, concentrating on each and every step to avoid a broken hip, or, in my case, a broken bag of water. I treated my midsection like the Hope Diamond encased in glass at the Smithsonian Museum. It contained a rare treasure worth millions of dollars.

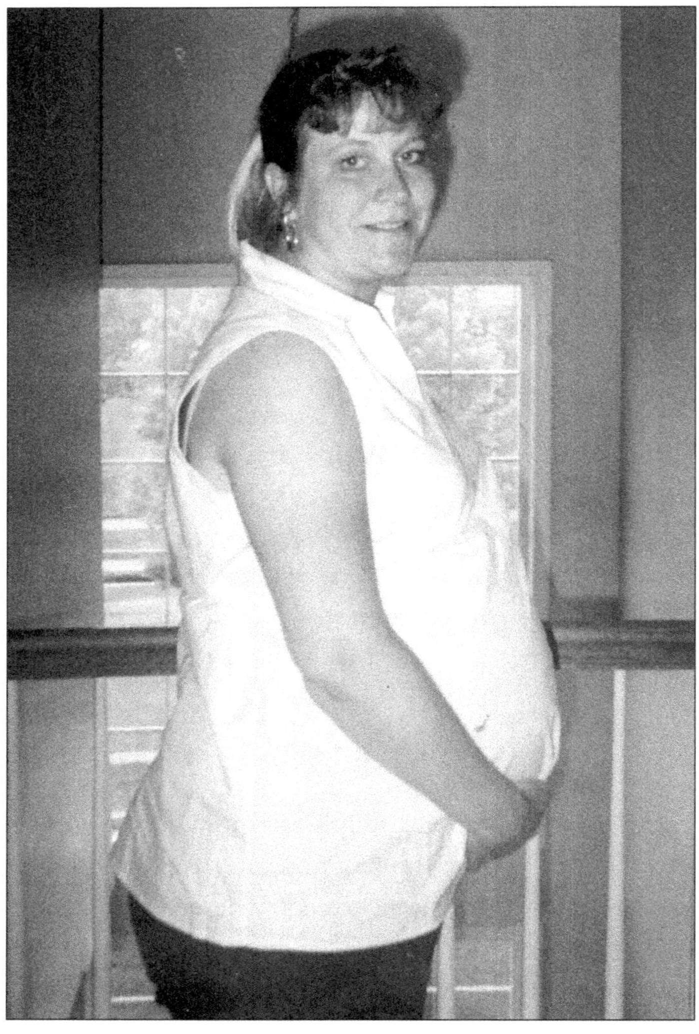

The author at twenty-seven weeks plus five days pregnant

As all eyes drew to me, I felt like a celebrity on the red carpet (even though I looked like a gargantuan lemon in my yellow maternity top). This was my moment to shine, and shine I did. Meri, my friend and biggest advocate on the baby-making front, helped my fifteen-year-old daughter, Deborah, organize the baby shower.

At nearly forty years old, eight-and-a-half months pregnant, and with a weight gain of forty-plus pounds, I had the energy level of an end-stage heart failure patient. Accordingly, I planted myself on the couch like a medicine ball plopped in the mud. I hoisted my body out of the recesses of the sofa only for important reasons, like when nature called or to greet a guest I had not seen in umpteen years.

The turnout was stellar; friends trickled out of the woodwork to attend this event. I suppose they sensed this baby shower was a victorious ceasefire to the battle that raged within me for four years. This was my equivalent of a presidential inaugural ball.

I exchanged small talk with friends both new and from the past. "I couldn't believe how tall the trees have grown when I was driving into the neighborhood," said Beth, my childhood friend from age eight to eighteen who grew up next door to me. She came from a spirited household with four children, two dogs, and a cat. There was a strong sense of community in that house, and I always wanted to conjure that up for myself when I had a family of my own. With baby number three in my belly (and two cats at home), I was well on my way.

I salivated like a steady plumbing leak as I gazed at the three-tiered cake smothered in sky-blue icing, scattered with tiny red hearts, and bordered in white frosting. A confectionary brown woven basket containing a smiling baby perched atop the second tier and a blue, yellow, and pink balloon each sprouted out of the top. A white strip of ribbon draped out of the basket and down the side of the cake with the inscription "Destination Rhodes House." I could not wait for the sugar rush of the first spongy, sweet mouthful.

As I released the ribbon and tore the wrapping paper from each gift, blue sprang out from every direction; I had not kept it a secret that I was expecting a boy.

❧

I did, however, feel like a pilot of a weather plane in the eye of a hurricane, existing in a transient state of calm that could shift at any second with a turn of the wind, danger lurking at the fringes. When I harbored these thoughts, I reminded myself that my five-year-old daughter was praying every single night before bed that her baby brother would be safe.

I encountered a few minor cracks in the pavement, but nothing that threatened to steer my elation off course.

Wednesday, July 7, 2004

I've gotten a couple of leg cramps in my calves upon waking in the morning. The second one was the worst pain I've ever experienced, and it was sore for four days (although it wasn't swollen). I have read that calf cramps are common during pregnancy. Hope this helps.

Sunday, July 18, 2004

I have awful heartburn with this pregnancy (and my other two). It usually starts later in the afternoon, and I take up to three doses of Tums (three Tums at a time) a day.

I've been consistently having heartburn every day for the past couple of months. It's really bad at about 10:00 at night when I lie down in bed, and it also wakes me up most nights between 2:00 a.m. and 4:00 a.m. It's so bad it makes me feel sick, and I actually threw up from the heartburn on one occasion. I have taken a lot of Tums with this pregnancy and my two other living children's pregnancies, and it didn't do any harm....

❧

I entered the homestretch and ached to meet my long-awaited son. Most women bemoan the trials of pregnancy: the moodiness, lethargy, morning sickness, heartburn, leg cramps, stretch marks, hugeness, limitations, and more. I must be a glutton for punishment, but I reveled in every one of these aggravating symptoms, as they all personified carrying a new life.

Almost all women lament the loss of their figure as they start expanding. I welcomed it with open arms, was proud of it, wanted to be as big as a mansion so the world would know my news just by looking at me.

Every little flutter and kick fascinated me to no end, and my favorite pastime was lying in bed each night and "watching the show" as the frolicsome little life force made my stomach roll in waves while I observed in awe.

Sunday, July 18, 2004

I'll be thirty-seven weeks pregnant on Tuesday and am anxiously awaiting my scheduled C-section (on 7/29). Only ten days to go from tomorrow. I can't wait! On my last doctor's visit, my cervix was soft but not dilated.

Have been having a lot of Braxton Hicks contractions. Can't wait to meet this little guy (actually, most likely, big guy). My last baby (girl) weighed 10 lbs. 8 oz. at birth (was four days overdue). I figure since they're taking this one two wks. early that he'll weigh a measly 9 lbs. or so. Ha Ha!

❧

Just to make sure I did not bask in my brief worry-free existence, I woke up one night around a week before my scheduled C-section with what felt like a near-death experience. I jolted from unconsciousness to consciousness with a horrifying realization that I could not take in air. My wretched heartburn (which I later found out was acid reflux) caused vomit to be expelled upward as I slept. I shot into an upright position faster than any nine-months-pregnant woman in history and shoved Mark awake, clutching at my throat, the universal choking signal. He registered alarm, and two smacks between the shoulder blades later, I inhaled a renewing breath. Thank God Mark was beside me when this happened, or the baby and I may have expired on the spot from a freak accident. I was afraid to go to sleep at night after this "pleasant" event and piled my head and shoulders up on pillows before the lights went out.

The new choking-to-death-in-my-sleep worry coupled with its faithful companion, fear of cord accident (umbilical cord wrapping around the baby's neck in utero), made me want this baby out *yesterday.*

CHAPTER 10

Matthew's Birth Story

With God all things are possible.
~MATTHEW 19:26

The much-anticipated day arrived. It was July 29, 2004, thirteen days before I was due. My due date of August 11 was my daughter Ally's birthday, which was ironic. My doctor and I decided to take the baby early because of his large size, my increasing discomfort, and to alleviate my fears—to get him here alive before disaster struck. I was a pressure cooker of worry after all my unfortunate scenarios. I believed if there was even a remote chance that something bad could happen, it would, as the events of my life from the last few years resembled the consequences of an unanswered chain letter.

We were due at Fairfax Hospital, Women and Children's Center, by 9:00 a.m., with the scheduled C-section set for 10:30 a.m. I am not exaggerating—I never even dozed for a moment the night before; I was apprehensive, so sleep was not in the equation. I had anticipated this day for *four years*. My mother spent the night so she could stay home with Deborah and Ally while we were at the hospital.

We took the elevator upstairs to labor and delivery since I was preregistered. We proceeded to a waiting room with other mothers in queue for delivery. I have hypoglycemia, so I prayed I wouldn't faint before the procedure. It was as silent as a museum in the room due to the collective nerves of all the mothers-in-waiting. I found it difficult to sit in comfort because of my large girth. I sat in a rocking chair when it became available but found no relief; it was as hard as a cutting board. Time was interminable; we waited two hours before they called us.

A nurse examined me in an area with curtained-off partitions. She strapped the external fetal monitor to my abdomen to monitor the baby's heart rate. It fell within normal range much to my relief. The nurse was a bubbly, talkative woman who explained everything that was about to happen to me with the cesarean. I was a little concerned about the anesthesia, since with my prior C-section, the numbing effect went all the way up to my neck. I felt like I could not control my own breathing, creating panic. She assuaged my fears by telling me that since I was having a spinal this time versus an epidural, they were better able to target the area to be numbed. She proceeded to administer the IV onto the top of my right hand. She said it would be easier to hold the baby with the IV in this location. Of all the IV's I've had in my life, this was by far the most painful one. It felt like a piece of wood was shoved into my vein. I thought, *If I can survive this, the caesarean will be a piece of cake.* I voiced concerns over my acid reflux and my near-drowning-in-my-own-vomit experience a couple of weeks ago. She called in the anesthesiologist, who handed me a vile-tasting Zantac cocktail, assuring me this would prevent the reflux while on the operating table.

At around 11:30 a.m., I was told it was time to begin the procedure. I was surprised when they motioned me to walk to the operating room on my own since I was strapped with a myriad of gadgets. It was difficult to walk. I felt like an oversized penguin waddling down the hall with my rear end trying to escape out of the back of my flimsy gown. All modesty would be required to go by the wayside as there were more important items of business to deal with.

The operating room was luminous and sterile. The nurses/orderlies hoisted me onto the operating table. They asked me my weight and I was mortified. "I weigh a lot," I said with remorse.

"Don't worry," one of them said. "We've had a lot heavier." *Was this supposed to make me feel better?* I felt like a circus sideshow seated up there with all eyes on the fat lady.

The anesthesiologist entered and told me to curl up over the side of the table (no easy feat), and they administered the spinal anesthesia. I do not recall any pain—just a little sting. They told me to lie down right away since the numbness would start to take effect in no time. They said that with a spinal, I would be able to feel touch but no pain. At this point, my husband came into the operating room, donned in scrubs and a surgical mask. He looked like an MD. The anesthetic worked down low and not all the way up to my neck like it had with Ally's delivery (which made me feel like I was suffocating). That was a relief. I was able to relax and breathe without effort.

It seemed that no time at all passed before I heard a lusty cry. What a joyous sound that was to my ears. Some babies have temporary breathing difficulties after a C-section due to not coming down the birth canal, but apparently mine did not. My miracle entered the world at 12:18 p.m. They carried my baby over to the warming table across the room. I looked over and saw the most beautiful sight of my life, a white-haired angel. His hair glowed like a beacon. The whole scenario was surreal; I could not take my eyes off him as they welled up with tears. I felt an intoxicating joy; sunlight flooded my heart. God smiled upon me at that moment.

Ever since I was a little girl, Matthew was my name of choice for any future son. The youngest brother of Beth Boyd, my good friend next door, was named Matthew, and I liked the way that traditional name sounded when it passed over my lips. My father's first name, Thomas, was already taken by Matthew's predecessor (my first unborn son). I thought it would be acceptable to borrow it as the middle name in honor of my father and Tommy, who were both watching over us. Thus, Matthew Thomas was named. Soon after I discovered I was pregnant with another boy, I perused a book on baby names and their backgrounds. I was shocked and touched to unearth the meaning of the name Matthew: Gift from God. How providential that I'd chosen this name thirty years earlier.

One of the nurses handed my baby to me, and I asked her if it was okay to hold him in my morphine-induced haze. I feared I might drop him. She said that yes, the mother must hold the baby as she was wheeled from the OR to the recovery room. I thanked my doctor, Dr. Samuel Grimes, as I rolled past him on the way out.

In the recovery room, I handed Matthew to my husband so that he would be in safe hands. A nurse came in and placed warming blankets on me, and I remember being in a state of pure bliss. I felt pride as the doctor came by to congratulate me on the birth of my son. My husband told me that our boy weighed a hefty 9 pounds 11 ounces, rather substantial for being two weeks early.

The next several hours were a blur; the anesthesiologist had added a long-acting twenty-four-hour dose of morphine to the spinal. Matthew spent the night in the nursery since I was "high" on morphine and did not trust myself to handle him. I was so congested that night that I woke up from my own snoring on several occasions. *My poor roommate.* I still had a catheter in, so I was able to lie in bed until the next morning. I was not in any pain whatsoever.

The morning following the birth, the hospital photographer came by to take Matthew's newborn picture. My little angel opened his eyes for his first photograph, as if he realized the significance of the first photo shoot.

The hospital took this picture when Matthew was one day old. His proud oldest sister, Deborah, held him for this shot. I like to think that starry light to the left of them is God shining down, sharing in the miracle of his existence.

Matthew, one day old, with sister Deborah, age fifteen

My brother, Tim, and his girlfriend, Donna, visited later that morning, and I felt like a partygoer at Woodstock. I was really out of it from the drugs they gave me, laughing at the silliest things. I do not recall much of their visit.

My first roommate was a single Latino woman. I felt her loneliness through the dividing curtain, as she had no guests whatsoever. My partition was full of visitors and laughter, and I felt sad for her situation, guilty for our revelry.

By afternoon of the day after Matthew's birth, the morphine wore off, and the pain set in like a ton of lead weights. Just shifting positions in the bed was excruciating. I took Percocet every four hours to make the agony somewhat manageable. My first trek to the bathroom after the catheter removal was a journey of pain and will. I leaned on my husband every step of the way. I was relieved I did not have the rigid abdomen and vomiting issues that I had experienced following my previous C-section with Ally.

The newborn heel prick to check for certain disorders, such as phenylketonuria (PKU) tore at my heartstrings. This evoked a great deal of pain accompanied by screaming from Matthew. I knew the pokes were for his own good, but they nonetheless put me on the brink of new-mother's tears.

Another equally grueling procedure was the circumcision. Being the mother of two girls, I was not prepared for this. When the doctor swooped my little boy away to perform this male rite of passage, it was more upsetting to me than I realized it would be. The thought of the doctor cutting off a portion of my baby boy's private parts while he was awake seemed barbaric; I felt guilty for signing off on something so cruel. When the staff returned Matthew to me after the procedure, he was screaming like a banshee, and I immediately nursed him, which calmed him down. *My poor boy.*

Since I did not elect to get a private room, Mark was not allowed to spend the night; I was on my own. By the second night, I was expected to walk to the bathroom, a monumental task without the aid of a spouse. Panic set in as visiting hours ended and Mark left for the night. I managed to tackle my nightly bathroom visits by hugging the rolling IV pole for dear life on the journey. My advice to anyone who is scheduled for a C-section would be to score a private room so her husband/significant other can stay in the room overnight.

Late in the afternoon the next day, my Percocet wearing off, I buzzed the nurse for more painkiller. Twenty minutes passed, and still no sign of the nurse. I buzzed again, and she said she would be there soon. "Soon" turned into sixty minutes that passed in slow motion, and by the time she arrived, the pain was unbearable. I was in tears. I sobbed and gripped the IV pole for dear life as I stumbled to the bathroom. My older daughter, Deborah, who was visiting me then and feeling emotional because she needed to leave for the beach the next morning with her father and his family, began to cry. I regretted that she saw me like that. I vowed then and there if I ever became a labor and delivery nurse (I have toyed with the idea), I would respond swiftly to the pain relief requests of new mothers.

My milk came in on Saturday, and my breasts were so engorged that I felt like Violet from *Willie Wonka and the Chocolate Factory* after she blew up like a blueberry. The hot, stinging pain was assuaged when the angel of mercy (the night nurse) so kindly demonstrated how to use the double electric breast pump, every lactating mother's new best friend.

Matthew took to nursing like a champ, which was a plus. Nursing is similar to riding a bike—if you have successfully mastered it with the first child, odds are you will get the hang of it without much trouble with the next. It is amazing what the doctors proclaim are safe drugs to take when nursing (morphine and Percocet, to name a couple), as these medications pass straight to the baby through the milk. I checked with the doctor twice before I believed him. He probably thought I was hard of hearing. After going through nine months of pregnancy screening everything that entered my mouth for safety, it went against my better judgment to do this. However, my baby was hungry and needed to eat.

Roommate number two was a woman who had just delivered her fourth child, and her baby had jaundice. I recall hearing her concerned conversations with her husband regarding bilirubin lights and insurance coverage issues. I snored heavily that night (like a rhino), and was embarrassed when I passed her curtained partition en route to the bathroom.

Matthew spent every night in the nursery, as my pain was intense and lifting him was insurmountable. Every time I went to retrieve him from the nursery, I felt guilt around the nurses, like they thought I was a negligent mother. The nursery staff informed me that Matthew did not sleep much in the bassinet and cried and woke up the other babies at night. *Great*, I thought—*my little troublemaker.*

The day of discharge, a Sunday three days after Matthew's birth, was a stressful one (*Is anything ever easy for me?* I wondered). It started out with a bleed in the circumcision area that I discovered during a diaper change. I paged the nurse right away, and she applied silver nitrate to stop the bleeding. I was afraid it would happen again after we were home and without medical assistance.

The next issue we faced was the news that our son had developed a mild case of jaundice. Matthew would not be required to lay under the bilirubin lights, however. The jaundice gave him a ruddy appearance, like a little lobster. The doctor told us to get the bilirubin levels checked a couple of days later and to monitor his coloring and notify them right away if the whites of his eyes turned yellow.

A couple of hours prior to our release, Matthew began a screaming jag out of the blue. Nothing I attempted would comfort him, which brought out frustration and worry on my part. My baby wailed away as I was wheeled down the corridor from my room. The nurse stopped by the nursery to change his diaper one final time, and when she returned, she told me how he fought it and said, "Boy, he sure is strong!" *The strongest of all five embryos that were placed into me; he is the warrior,* I thought. I like to think Matthew was the fifth embryo I insisted on putting in.

Thankfully, Matthew's circumcision site stopped bleeding, and his jaundice resolved on its own. After a laborious road, I brought home a robust, healthy baby—a miracle to me.

This would be unwelcome news for First Response, whose stock price would now be sure to plummet.

Tuesday, August 3, 2004

Just a quick note to let you know that Matthew Thomas Rhodes arrived by scheduled C-section on Thursday, July 29 at 12:18 p.m., weighing in at a hefty 9 lbs. 11 oz. and 20½ inches long (at two weeks early!) His Apgars were 9 and 9. He has a beautiful head of light-blond hair and is an absolute angel. I will send a birth story when I get more time and am not so exhausted.

CHAPTER 11

Icing on the Cake

Heaven is home. Utopia is here. Nirvana is now.
~Edward Abbey

Years later, as we drove down Route 50 on the Saturday before Mother's Day in 2008 for the third annual GIVF Baby Reunion, my three children tried to guess what the stuffed animal would be that year. "Will it be a panda, a hippo, a kangaroo?" Ally asked with excitement in her voice.

"I can't wait for the buffet," said my nineteen-year-old daughter, Deborah. She woke up early on a Saturday morning (an amazing occurrence) because she did not want to miss this. My three-year-old son, my IVF baby, had been asking me daily, "How many days till we see the clowns, mommy?"

The greeters beamed at us from the sign-in table where we picked up our name tags. The smiling woman handed my children the anticipated stuffed animal, which turned out to be a teddy bear that year.

As I entered the expansive room, my chest seized and my eyes started to well up with tears; I was overcome with emotion. Since my first infertility appointment at GIVF, my dream had been to attend one of these reunions. Gathered in the event room of the Fairview Marriott Hotel in Falls Church, Virginia, were hundreds of parents whose wishes had been realized, who had lived through the gut-wrenching ache for a child who yesterday was only conceived in their dreams. I knew their pain and their ecstasy.

The room was a dazzling cacophony of babies' and toddlers' singsong chorus, school-aged children's carefree glee, and the calmer acceptance of older children and even the occasional college-aged child that they were conceived in a unique and thoughtful manner. Bursts of balloons clustered like molecules, interspersed throughout the ceiling in brilliant hues of soft lavender, bright pink, baby blue, lime green, and all the colors of pure happiness. The clowns juggled to the delight of the children; the face painters etched elaborate designs, from beautiful butterflies to baseballs and bats, on children's faces. A glass cabinet set up on a side wall contained an assortment of stuffed animals from reunions past: giraffes, ducks, and tigers, among others. This room was a microcosm of heaven.

The speakers strode to the podium with dignity and pride; the CEO introduced the founder of this successful enterprise, retired but still attending this celebration of life once a year, jubilant in the fact that he brought new life to so many. My eyes filled as I recognized the doctor onstage who thread my five embryos into me.

I looked down upon my son, almost four years old, with snow-white blond hair and blue eyes, and if ever I doubted my purpose in this universe, it dissolved. I had much to be thankful for on this Mother's Day weekend.

I witnessed a remarkable transformation in my husband after Matthew's birth. His initial lack of enthusiasm about having another baby had been difficult to bear, but he came around in the end.

Mark with Matthew, age nine months

Thursday, June 17, 2004

First of all, congratulations on your pregnancy. I hope all the testing goes well and produces good results. I can completely relate to your comments about your DH's attitude toward the pregnancy. I am thirty-nine (will be forty in Oct.), and my DH is forty. I'm in my thirty-third week of pregnancy with a healthy baby boy (had amnio). We have two children already (girls, five and fifteen). He has always been negative about having a third child. I've felt like I've had to carry the excitement over the pregnancy all myself (well, my girls are also excited). Yes, it is a lonely feeling when your DH doesn't share your enthusiasm. My DH just didn't "get it" when I told him that I needed to try to have another healthy baby after my AHC for tri 13 in Jan. 2001 (I've had five early M/Cs since my AHC before finally hitting the jackpot with this baby). He makes comments all the time, like "I won't retire till I'm eighty now" or "our lives will be over when the baby comes." I know he will love the baby when he sees him, but it makes the pregnancy very stressful with his attitude about it. He has only been to the first sonogram (I've had six) and says that he can't take off any more work to come) and when I try to get him to feel the baby kicking, he just acts like I'm bothering him and says it makes him feel squeamish to feel him kicking. I wish he could share my excitement, and we get in many fights about this. But you know what? Don't let his attitude spoil your excitement. I'm excited for you. If you ever need to talk, I'm here, as I totally understand.

❧

On a warm fall day in 2009, I looked out the window over the kitchen sink to see father and son in the backyard pitching baseballs to each other. Their baseball caps were turned backward, giving Mark the innocent and boyish appearance of Opie from the *Andy Griffith Show*. They looked like twins with their matching caps and blond hair. When Matthew looks in the mirror, his dad's pictures from toddlerhood are reflected; the resemblance is uncanny.

Five-year-old Matthew slammed the plastic ball over the fence and stared open-mouthed at his accomplishment.

"Whoa—you hit it outta the park, Matt," said his dad, his pride revealed in his wide smile.

I walked downstairs to the basement to find myself an intruder in a boys' club. Father and son were sitting with legs splayed out on the floor in front of the wide-screen television. There were bright-colored race cars whizzing around the track as the announcer informed that Jimmy Johnson made a pit stop due to a blown tire. "Oh, man," said Matthew, "now he won't be in second place."

A mandatory platter sat between them, housing Lay's potato chips, Helluva Good dip, slices of sharp cheddar cheese atop saltines, and Pepsi. My husband, who before my son's obsession with race cars never thought to include Nascar racing in his sports repertoire, has become an avid fan.

Father and son share a love of sports and can also be found watching baseball, football, basketball, or wrestling together several times a week.

One night, as Mark and I checked in on Matthew while he slept, I saw his eyes lingering on his son and asked him, "How much do you love him?"

"Words can't even describe it," he answered, and then he added, "Thank you for having him."

Hard to imagine this was the same man, who, a few years before, would rather tear a rotator cuff than have another child, who I feared might never forgive me for railroading him into this; at that point, I realized all was well.

Before Matthew's birth, cruel floodgates were behind my eyes and ready to spill over at any time. Today, I still have tears behind my eyes, but they are now full of joy, like dew on an early fall morning.

CHAPTER 12

Gifts and Lessons Learned

Judge your success by what you had
to give up in order to get it.
~Dalai Lama

I used to wonder why all these abysmal things happened to me in succession after the year 2000 ended. I pondered God's reasons for all the pain. Now that I can sit back with 20/20 vision and view the entire fiasco, I have clarity.

The first thing I learned is that everything is not black and white; there are gray areas that can only be discovered when you live through them. I used to be a hard and judging person in my early twenties. I took the Myers-Briggs Type Indicator (MBTI) test, a psychological profile that measures personality, during that time period. My results revealed that I am an INTJ, which means I tend to be an introvert, intuitive, thinking, and judging. I swung far to the right on the judging score. I believe it was accurate at the time; I spouted my opinions about abortion on several occasions, which was easy to do when never faced with the harsh reality of that devastating scenario. I think if I retook the test now, the score would be softened. I've since gained compassion and the willingness to step back and try to view a situation through another person's lens.

The second lesson will sound like a cliché, but good

old-fashioned perseverance *can* pay off. I focused on my quest with the relentlessness and obsession of a prizefighter. After each miscarriage, I would convince myself I was done trying, but that thought was short-lived. The multiple losses became so familiar that the nerve endings of my emotions were desensitized, like after receiving an injection of a numbing agent. I became a mechanical doll, a bobblehead getting punched in the face time after time and settling back into place. My mantra became "If at first you don't succeed, try, try again." If you have a goal or dream, do not let others dissuade you. If you believe it in your core, go for it; forge ahead. Nothing is gained from sitting on the sidelines.

Third, I think this series of adversities happened for a greater purpose. I have evolved into a compassionate and stronger person through Tommy's brief existence and my five subsequent miscarriages. My experiences have cultivated an empathy for hardship and a camaraderie that I can use to relate to others' suffering. It opened a door to my heart and unleashed the words, pen to paper, that could act as a balm to another person enduring the pain that I did during those four years. Chronicling my experience has been cleansing and therapeutic. If just one person is comforted and encouraged by reading it, then its worth has been realized.

The fourth point is more a gift than a lesson learned. I am a stronger person because of what happened. I figure if I can live through this, I can deal with just about anything (and I *have*). As an aside, since Matthew's birth in the summer of 2004, I have dealt with numerous other calamities. These include Mark's brother dying of alcoholism at the age of thirty-three in May 2005; two endometrial biopsies to rule out uterine cancer (each with three-week waits for the results—an eternity), which were negative, thank God; an orbital tumor (a cavernous hemangioma, or blood vessel tumor) in my left eye socket pressing on my optic nerve, which required surgery at Johns Hopkins to remove it in March 2006, a bad asthma attack requiring a 911 call followed by an all-nighter at the hospital in March 2007 for my eldest daughter, Deborah; my career as an accountant being put to rest, after passing three out of four of the CPA exams, due to an ischemic stroke that happened October 23, 2015, which has left me with short-term memory loss; a hole in my heart (the cause of my stroke) that was surgically closed in December 2015, and a diagnosis of alpha-gal syndrome (an allergy to red meat) in September 2017, the result of a tick bite that caused anaphylaxis (my throat to close) on two occasions, sending me to the emergency room. Nothing I can't handle, though. The good times keep on comin', and I have to roll with the punches.

A table of some of my major traumatic events follows with the silver lining(s):

EVENTS	GIFTS
Dad's sudden cardiac arrest and death at age 48 when I was 20 years old	Made me stronger and able to relate to others going through this
My clinical depression since 1988	More empathetic toward others
Divorce in 1993 from first husband	Birth of my first daughter, Deborah
Trisomy 13 termination (1/18/01)	Learned not to judge others if you haven't gone through a similar situation

EVENTS	GIFTS
5 miscarriages (2001–2003)	Made me a stronger person and led to Matthew's birth
Cavernous hemangioma (causing a small blind spot in central vision of the eye)	Was not malignant
Ischemic stroke (October 2015)	Do not take anything for granted; about 98 percent recovered
CPA shot down when 3/4 completed	Got to spend more time with Matthew; the satisfaction that I passed 3/4 of the exams
Atrial septal defect (hole in back of heart)	Skipping heartbeats fixed when surgically closed
Alpha-gal (anaphylactic allergy to red meat) diagnosed in September 2017	Lost weight; eat health er now

I have gained the incentive to "pay it forward." I feel blessed; I am healthy; and I want to push my good fortune ahead to others. To that end, during Christmas 2008, I sponsored a foster child. I shopped for festive clothing, candy, electronics, and other goodies for a seventeen-year-old girl who was in need. Giving back rewarded my heart and nourished my spirit. Then, I received an email from the Red Cross stating that they were in critical need of platelet donors during the holidays and that a donation might enable a cancer patient to leave the hospital and visit home for Christmas. I made the appointment and arrived at Inova Donor Services in Centreville, Virginia, at 2:00 p.m. on Christmas Eve. An IV, chills, and two hours of my time never felt so good. The technician retrieved double platelets and red blood cells. As I was leaving, she said, "You saved three lives today."

"That feels good," I said.

૭૩

Every time my husband asked what I wanted for my birthday, Christmas, wedding anniversary, or Valentine's Day, I wished for a baby; every time I blew out a birthday candle, I wished for a baby; every time I snapped my side of the wishbone and won, I wished for a baby.

It is ironic that Mark's health insurance at AOL stopped offering infertility coverage soon after Matthew's birth. The timing was impeccable, like a late car sliding onto the ferry just before the gate closes. I opened the oyster to find a pearl when, after four years of trying, Matthew was born in July 2004; a light switch in my soul flicked on. Before his birth, I had been moving through my life in a state of mild (and sometimes moderate) depression, but I acquired a contentment and happiness I had never experienced after I won the long battle. Every day is Christmas in my house since Matthew was born. Children and family are what are important in life; they are a gift from God and should be cherished every moment we are blessed with them. I still get tears in my eyes at least once a day when I look at my son and realize that my family is now complete with three dearly loved children. I am the luckiest person alive.

Finally, my faith has been restored because of this long-running, strenuous journey. I never pinpointed what "worked," never discovered the cause, do not know if it was the IVF or prayer or just "luck," but I am leaning toward prayer. I have also learned to truly appreciate the miracle that I bore two healthy, beautiful daughters who are the lights of my life. My perspective on life has changed 100 percent, and I no longer take anything for granted. I consider my children a gift.

One evening when Matthew was three years old, I had this conversation with my nine-year-old daughter, Ally, as we lay in my bed.

Ally: "Do you believe in magic?"

Me: "No, but I believe in miracles."

Ally: "Me, too. Matthew Thomas Rhodes, he told me that miracles can happen."

Me: "When? Today?"

Ally: "When he was born."

That says it all.

Acknowledgments

I would like to thank my husband, Mark, my daughters, Deborah and Ally, and my son, Matthew, for their patience while I spent countless hours writing this book over the last several years. A special thanks also goes out to my cheerleaders, my mother, Peggy Harris, and my dear friend Meri Greene, who provided constant inspiration to bring my story to fruition. I am also appreciative of my editor, Candace Johnson, for her invaluable guidance and enthusiasm for my story. Lastly, I am grateful to Genetics and IVF Institute for offering me the technological advances to bring my son into the world.

Terms and Acronyms

AF—"Aunt Flo"; menstrual period.

AFP—alpha-fetoprotein; a protein made by liver and yolk sac of developing fetus and normally found in fetal blood, usually between sixteen and eighteen weeks.

AHC—A Heartbreaking Choice; website supporting women who have undergone termination of pregnancy for medical reasons. Also the term for a pregnancy termination due to fetal anomalies.

Amnio—amniocentesis; medical procedure where small amount of amniotic fluid is sampled from amniotic sac surrounding developing fetus to check for genetic disorders or chromosomal abnormalities (for example, Down syndrome). Performed between fourteen and sixteen weeks gestation. Also determines sex of baby.

Apgar—scored test to quickly summarize health of newborn against infant mortality. Determined by rating newborn health on five simple criteria (appearance, pulse, grimace, activity, and respiration) on scale from zero to two, then summing up the five values obtained. Score ranges from zero to ten.

BCP—birth control pill.

Braxton Hicks Contractions—intermittent uterine contractions ("practice contractions") that can start as early as second trimester of pregnancy but more common in third trimester.

Uterine muscles tighten for approximately thirty to sixty seconds, sometimes for as long as two minutes.

Chemical pregnancy—early miscarriage that occurs by fifth week of gestation.

CI-AHC—a message board for supporting women who have conception issues after a pregnancy termination due to fetal anomalies.

Clomid—clomiphene citrate; oral medication to stimulate ovulation, used for irregular ovulation, unexplained infertility, and to improve timing of insemination with woman's cycle when there are "male factor" fertility issues.

Clomid challenge test (CCCT)—infertility blood test administers fertility drug Clomid and measures increases in levels of follicle stimulating hormone (FSH) and luteinizing hormone (LH). Determines whether adequate eggs can be made for in vitro fertilization (IVF).

CM—cervical mucus; type of cervical fluid produced right before ovulation, during time when most fertile.

D&C—dilation and curettage; dilation of cervix and surgical removal of part of lining of uterus and/or contents of uterus by scraping. Used to diagnose and treat heavy uterine bleeding, or to clear uterine lining after miscarriage or abortion.

D&E—dilation and evacuation; procedure performed in second twelve weeks (second trimester) of pregnancy to evacuate uterus of fetal and placental tissue with combination of suction and instruments.

DH—dear husband (or damned husband).

DPO—days past ovulation.

E2—estrogen; primary female sex hormone responsible for

primary development and regulation of female reproductive system and secondary sex characteristics.

EDD—estimated date of delivery.

embie—embryo; unborn child until end of seventh week following conception.

Endometrial biopsy—removal of small tissue sample from lining of uterus sent to lab to be looked at under microscope and tested for abnormal cells. Evaluates luteal phase of woman undergoing infertility evaluation. Determines if ovulation occurred and whether uterine lining has undergone changes necessary for implantation of fertilized egg and support of early pregnancy.

Estrogen—any group of steroid hormones that promote development and maintenance of female characteristics of body during menstrual cycle. Produces environment suitable for fertilization, implantation, and nutrition of early embryo.

FISH—fluorescent in situ hybridization; study of sperm chromosome to check for male factor infertility.

FSH—follicle stimulating hormone; regulates development, growth, pubertal maturation, and reproductive processes of female body. Initiates growth of ovarian follicles.

GIVF—Genetics and IVF Institute (located in Fairfax, Virginia).

Gonal-F—injectable fertility drug that induces ovulation. Naturally occurring hormone used to stimulate a follicle (egg) to develop and mature.

h/b—heartbeat (of fetus).

hCG (or Beta)—human chorionic gonadotropin; pregnancy

hormone made by cells formed in placenta, which nourishes egg after fertilization and becomes attached to uterine wall.

hpt—home pregnancy test.

HSG—hysterosalpingogram; female fertility test where dye injected into uterine cavity through vagina and cervix to see if fallopian tubes open or blocked.

ICSI—intracytoplasmic sperm injection; procedure where quality sperm chosen and injected directly into cytoplasm of mature egg. Specialized form of IVF for male factor infertility.

IUI—intrauterine insemination; fertility treatment where sperm placed inside woman's uterus to facilitate fertilization.

IVF—in vitro fertilization; process of extracting eggs, retrieving sperm sample, and then manually combining egg and sperm in laboratory dish for fertilization. Embryo then transferred to uterus.

Level 3 U/S—advanced anatomic detailed ultrasound where existence of all fetal organs verified and abnormalities in anatomical structure ruled out.

Lupron—leuprolide acetate; hormone used in conjunction with FSH in IVF. Inhibits pituitary gland's ability to control ovary and used to reduce likelihood of unintended ovulation during assisted reproduction cycles.

Luteal phase defect (LPD)—when ovaries don't release enough progesterone to make lining of uterus grow, or lining of uterus doesn't respond to hormone, associated with both infertility and early miscarriage.

M/C—miscarriage.

OB—obstetrician; doctor who studies pregnancy, childbirth, and postpartum period. (Also known as ob-gyn.)

OPK—ovulation predictor kit; tests woman's urine for surge in luteinizing hormone (LH), which happens a day or two before ovulation.

PG—pregnancy.

PGD—preimplantation genetic diagnosis; genetic profiling procedure used prior to implantation into uterus to help identify genetic defects within embryo. Embryos used in PGD are usually created during IVF.

Placenta previa—placenta partially or totally covers opening of cervix in pregnancy; can cause severe bleeding during pregnancy and delivery.

PREGLOSSAFTERAHC—pregnancy loss after AHC (termination).

Progesterone—hormone released by corpus luteum in ovary. Plays important role in menstrual cycle and in maintaining early stages of pregnancy.

Prolactin—protein that enables mammals and female humans to produce milk in breasts. High levels may inhibit ovulation and cause infertility.

Quad screen—blood test done in second trimester, usually between fifteen and twenty weeks pregnant, that tests for Down syndrome, trisomy 18 (Edwards syndrome), and neural tube defects such as spina bifida and anencephaly. Not a definitive test.

RE—reproductive endocrinologist; fertility specialist.

Repronex—drug consisting of mixture of follicle stimulating hormone (FSH) and luteinizing hormone (LH) to stimulate ovaries to produce eggs. Used to treat infertility.

SCSA—sperm chromatin structure assay; for males, determines percentage of sperm with high levels of DNA fragmentation, abnormal proteins, and morphology that inhibits fertilization.

Sonohysterogram—special type of ultrasound where fluid is put into uterus through cervix using thin plastic tube. Sound waves are then used to create images of lining of uterus.

SPD—online board for subsequent pregnancy discussion.

Sub-Q—subcutaneous.

Tri-18 or T-18—trisomy 18 (Edwards syndrome); severe chromosomal problem caused by an extra chromosome #18. Associated with severe intellectual disability and numerous physical abnormalities.

Tri-13 or T-13—trisomy 13 (Patau syndrome); severe chromosomal problem caused by an extra chromosome #13. Associated with severe intellectual disability and physical abnormalities in many parts of body.

Triple Screen—blood test used during second trimester of pregnancy to classify patient as either high risk or low risk for chromosomal abnormalities.

TTC—trying to conceive.

U/S—ultrasound; important first test for any woman having trouble conceiving. Examines uterus, ovaries, and endometrial lining. Also used during pregnancy to check fetal development.

2WW—two-week wait from time of intrauterine insemination (IUI) or in vitro fertilization (IVF) transfer to pregnancy test.

Support and Resources

A Time to Decide, a Time to Heal: For Parents Making Difficult Decisions about Babies They Love, Molly A. Minnick, MSW, Kathleen J. Delp, ACSW, Mary C. Ciotti, MD. Pineapple Press, 2000.
Written by mothers and fathers who have faced the news of a fetal anomaly with grief and courage.

Searching for the Stork: One Couples's Struggle to Start a Family, Marion Lee Wasserman. NAL Books, 1988.
A four-year "search for the stork," stillbirth, a rare genetic disorder, and their eventual adoption story.

Empty Arms: Coping with Miscarriage, Stillbirth and Infant Death, Sherokee Ilse. Wintergreen Press, 1996 (revised and enlarged edition 2015).
Reaches out to all who have been touched by infant death or miscarriage.

Precious Lives Painful Choices: A Prenatal Decision-Making Guide, Sherokee Ilse. Wintergreen Press, 1995.
Depicts aspects of continuing a pregnancy versus terminating a pregnancy when prenatal tests indicate a problem.

The Baby Void: My Quest for Motherhood, Judith Uyterlinde. Globe Pequot Press, 2008.
The journey from pregnancy losses to adoption.

About the Author

Suzanne Harris Rhodes has two BS degrees from George Mason University, one in information systems and the second in accounting. Her favorite pastimes include reading, writing, and researching medical topics. She has written numerous articles and published nine in *I Am Modern* magazine (a Northern Virginia publication), one of which is an article about IVF. *The Little Embryo That Could* is her first book.